WiFFLE BALL ®

BALL

The Ultimate Guide

Michael Hermann
with The Wiffle Ball, Inc.

TRIUMPH
BOOKS

Foul Line

Single Area

Foul Line

70-75 °

Home Run

95 FEET

Triple Area

65 FEET

ea

Wiffle Ball ®

The Ultimate Guide

Editors
Katy Sprinkel
Tony Puryear

Project manager
Perrie Briskin

Chief photographer
Christopher M. Lynch/Instilled Images

Illustrator
Ricardo Lopez

Key researchers
Zack Tawatari
Frances Callahan
Don Hermann

For Mom, Dad, and Lisa.

And, of course, for the Mullanys,
without whom none of this would be possible.

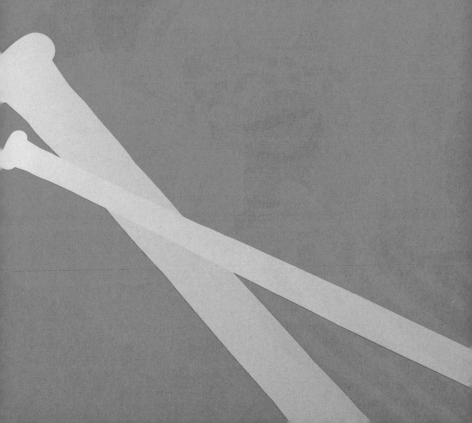

Dear Wiffle Enthusiasts,

Gathering information for this book on the beginnings of Wiffle has brought back fond memories of my childhood and working with my dad.

I've never forgotten his advice to me as we sat together at the kitchen table while trying to design the ball and formulate the rules and field layout for our game. He said, "Pay attention to the small things, Mull. Make sure they are correct the first time. The big things will take care of themselves."

How true his words have proven to be throughout my life.

Thank you, fans, for the support and interest in our family, company, and in Wiffle.

Best regards,

David A. Mullany

David A. Mullany
Co-creator of the Wiffle ball

Introduction

grew up in a noisy time. My childhood was filled with Merlin and 2-XL. *Bing, bang, buzz*—I was a kid of the '70s and I got used to my toys barking back at me. But amidst the blare, there was one toy that spoke its own magical language. One that made its own unique sound: That sweet sound of plastic on plastic. The sound of Wiffle ball.

That mystical eight-slotted white ball turned me into a magician each time I took the mound. The way that thing could swoop and swerve, there was nothing like it—and there still isn't.

What makes this game so special? Is it the beauty and simplicity of the Wiffle ball? Its easy connection to baseball? The memories? The fun?

Yes.

In the coming pages, I'm going to tell you a lot about that love for Wiffle and about the cult it's created. I mean, I knew there was a lot of Wiffle-love out there, but it wasn't until I traveled the country to see this stuff up close that I really understood.

I met a guy who bulldozed his backyard into a Fenway Park. I met a guy known simply as "Wiffman." I met a guy who bought his next-door neighbor's house in order to extend his own backyard Wiffle ball field. And I met a guy who can throw a Wiffle ball 95 miles per hour.

Who am I? I'm the guy who grew up loving Wiffle ball and who now gets to help oversee this great brand. I am president of a NYC-based brand management agency, Wicked Cow Entertainment. We manage The Wiffle Ball, Inc.'s brand initiatives. It's every bit as cool of a gig as it sounds. Before moving into brand management, I spent several years as a reporter and as a writer. But authoring this book is special. This is Wiffle ball, after all.

In the coming pages, you're going to read about how the game has transformed into a competitive sport. You're going to learn how to throw a riser, a knuckleball, a sinker, and a curve. You'll even get tips from the guys that get paid to do it. You'll get to know the Mullany family, inventors and creators of this beloved brand. You'll hear personal Wiffle ball memories from some of the biggest celebrities around. And you'll find the answers to that age-old question: How does a Wiffle ball do what it does?

Who's Palinczar? What's a Bernoulli? You'll soon know. *Wiffle Ball: The Ultimate Guide* is a one-of-a-kind look at how this astonishingly simple product has transformed lives. This book is filled with colorful characters and far-off Wiffle journeys.

The Wiffle ball has hardly changed over the years, yet its audience continues to grow. Our granddads have passed it to our fathers, our fathers to us, and we to our sons and daughters. Wiffle is still yellow, and white, red, white, and blue.

This is an ode to a great American brand, from one fan to another.

Pop Culture

1

It is perhaps the ultimate compliment America's collective pop consciousness can bestow: a brand becoming intermingled with the product it names.

In other words, a company makes a product so good, so memorable, that its own brand name becomes as recognizable as the product it produces.

Think of some of the great consumer brands of our time where the product and brand name became synonymous; you know 'em, you use 'em, you love 'em—adhesive bandages: Band-Aid; photocopy: Xerox; tissue: Kleenex; soda: Coke. The list doesn't stop there. There's Vaseline, Polaroid, Velcro, and Dixie Cups, to name a few.

And *everybody* knows baseball played with that yellow plastic bat and ball is called Wiffle ball. It is a testament to this enduring brand that Wiffle's name itself has become analogous with the game for which it was created—"Wiffle ball."

But make no mistake: Though Wiffle seems to be everywhere, it's a hallowed brand nearly 60 years standing. In other words, Wiffle = Wiffle™.

This American phenomenon continues to grow and reach new generations of fans. We've all played the game and chances are our kids and grandkids will play the game, too. How many things can you say that about?

Wiffle, with no moving parts, and featuring principles in physics that were new in 1738, is more popular than ever.

Wiffle has made an indelible mark on American culture since its inception nearly 60 years ago. From the early department stores where Wiffle was first sold, it has jumped off the shelves and into the hearts and minds (and yards, car trunks, gutters, and garages) of people across the country and around the world. You will find Wiffle ball played in parks, backyards, at charity events, on college campuses, and even in professional Wiffle leagues and tournaments.

VH1's *I Love Toys* ranks the Wiffle ball & bat the 10th best toy of all time

More impressive, all this has happened without a single penny spent on marketing since 1975. Wiffle's marketing budget is zero, nada, zip. Mattel, Coca-Cola, Hasbro, Disney, and other American megabrands have worked their way into our collective memories—but via multibillion-dollar marketing budgets. Wiffle is the rare brand these days that is truly organic, with people coming back year after year not because they saw a commercial or print ad, but because they love it. Because their dad played it when he was little. Because it gets people outside and interacting. Because nothing is more fun.

Wiffle has curved and swerved its way into books, paintings, and comic strips, not to mention television shows, movies, music, and video games. As a beloved piece of Americana, it has been enthusiastically referenced and increasingly revered.

It has become one of the most enduring toys in American history, one whose followers have a "devotion bordering on obsession," according to *The New York Times*.

VH1's special *I Love Toys* ranks the Wiffle ball and bat set as the 10th best toy of all time, between the Slinky (9) and Play Doh (11), leaving the Frisbee (45), Nerf (23), and even the bicycle (14) in the rearview mirror. The Hula Hoop, Barbie, and LEGO filled the top three

Julius Erving/Dr. J
NBA Legend

. . . On beating the stuffing out of a rival basketball team as a
10-year-old member of his Long Island Salvation Army team and
then getting his comuppance on the Wiffle ball field.

This had to be circa 1960, and I'm playing basketball for the Hempstead Salvation Army. We go to play a group of kids who belong to
the Glenville Baker Boys Club in Locust Valley.

We're the kids from Hempstead, and that year our squad probably played 50 basketball games. And we play this game and these
kids cannot score. I think the final score was 47–0. It's 47–0, and we
were even trying to let them score.

Suddenly it's over. And their coach [said to] our coach, "Well, let's
play a game of Wiffle ball since we've got all the kids here."

And we felt bad about beating them in basketball, so we set up a
game of Wiffle ball. And they [have] this kid who knows all the pitches.
So, like with a Wiffle ball, if you hold the ball a certain way, it rises, it
drops, it comes at you, it curves. Man, we couldn't hit this kid.

Next thing we turn around and the score is like 12–0. So they got
vindicated the same day we beat them 47–0 in basketball. They now
shut us out in Wiffle ball—nobody could hit the pitcher. The great
equalizer was the Wiffle ball.

. . . On his day at the plate.

I didn't get any hits. I couldn't hit him. I just remember that ball coming, and it was like, *whoosh, whoosh, whoosh.* It was wobbling. It was
like a flying saucer coming at you. And he would throw it right at you,
and it would come across the plate. They were much better Wiffle
ball players than they were basketball players, that's for sure.

4

slots; not bad company. The *New York Times* seconds that, proclaiming, "Wiffle ranks with Hula Hoop and Barbie as quintessentially American toys."

WIFFLE® BALL

Regulation

BASEBALL SIZE

And so says Tim Walsh, author of *The Playmakers*, a glossy history of the most influential toys of our time. "The Mullany family is so uncelebrated. If you create a piece of music that sells a million copies, they give you a gold record and put you on the cover of *Rolling Stone*." Walsh believes the Mullanys need their due. "They're still relatively unknown. [If] an album that sold as many copies as Wiffle has sold, well, [the Mullanys would] be as big as the Beatles or Michael Jackson."

Paradoxically, in the Age of the iPod and the video game, Wiffle, with no moving parts and featuring principles in physics that were new in 1738, is more popular than ever. It's everywhere. Wiffle balls and bats are sold in all 50 states and in dozens of countries. In the warm summer months, you can't walk into a store without seeing that familiar 24-count Wiffle display. It's in drugstores, it's in sporting goods stores, and it's in department stores.

To give you some idea of the iconic American-ness of this thing, here's a story from Hank Paine, owner of The Connecticut Store, which sells Connecticut products to customers worldwide. "We have a customer that orders [Wiffle products] in quantity and the only way to get them there is by Express Mail, so I end up standing in line at the post office. The guys are used to seeing me come over there.

After 1953, a suburban kid and a couple of friends could play a baseball game in his own backyard, with a ball that curved as if thrown by Dizzy Dean himself.

They'll say, 'Hey Hank, where are we going today?' And one day I answered, 'Well, we're going to send some made-in-Connecticut Wiffle balls to China.' There was a pause and the clerk looked at me and said, 'What'd you say?' I said, 'We're sending Wiffle balls to China.' He said, 'Holy crap, Hank, that's great,' and the people in back of me just started to applaud."

The appeal of this simple kids' toy cuts across ages and generations. They're playing Wiffle ball in backyards, they're playing it in schoolyards, they're playing at the South Pole, and they're playing it in Afghanistan. What's the deal? It's just an odd little ball and a yellow plastic bat. How did this unlikely duo get to be so popular? To answer that question, we need to go back to a different era, to 1953.

Pop culture exploded in the years following World War II. The 1950s were a relief from the Depression, the war that followed, and all of the rationing and stress that came along with both. The national mood had changed. It was the era of Marilyn Monroe, of fins on Cadillacs, and of Tupperware. Popular culture was evolving as the country healed from the war. *I Love Lucy*, *From Here to Eternity*, and Tony Bennett all topped their respective charts. It was a prosperous new era of mass production and mass consumption. The watchword was *buy*, *buy*, *buy* as standardized, branded consumables went mass-market, becoming more affordable than ever. 1953 saw the first color TVs, the first *TV Guides* to go with them, and the first Corvette automobiles.

Q

The year 1953 was a seminal year for which other brand?

It was a juncture of technological change that shifted the way people lived their daily lives. Injection molding, the process by which plastics are heated and shaped, was coming into its own. It allowed for products from milk cartons and combs to toothbrushes and garbage cans—anything plastic—to be produced more easily than ever before. It's no accident that the '50s was the age of simple injection-molded toys like the Hula Hoop and the Frisbee.

The fast food giant Mc Donald's, which opened its first franchise.

Perhaps most important, all these develop-ments were being fueled by the postwar baby boom. People were getting hitched and making babies in record numbers. They were moving out of cities. In response to this exodus, mass production hit the housing market too—with the advent of the G.I. Bill and with it the invention of the suburbs. As Levittowns sprouted, so did Wiffle balls and bats in those Levittowns' garages.

There is one last piece of our puzzle: The early '50s were also a golden age of baseball, with Yogi and The Mick taking the Yankees to their fifth consecutive world championship in 1953. That was also the year that the curveballing legend Dizzy Dean was inducted into the Hall of Fame. In 1953, America was baseball-crazy, the national pastime was at its postwar zenith, and here's the connection: baseball, the suburbs, *backyards*.

Before 1953, a kid could play baseball or stickball or stoopball. There was no plastic bat-and-ball set. It simply didn't exist. So get-ting a baseball game together was no easy feat.

IN THE BLEACHERS

© Steve Moore

| WIFFLE BALL | WIFFLE BAT | WIFFLE PLAYER |

7

It took a whole bunch of guys, for starters. You needed baseballs, gloves, and a backstop. And you needed a lot of room. So if you played it in, say, a suburban backyard, you were going to break every window on the block.

Wiffle balls and bats are sold in all 50 states and in dozens of countries.

And forget throwing a major-league curveball.

After 1953, a suburban kid and a couple of friends could play a baseball game in his own backyard, with a ball that curved as if thrown by Dizzy Dean himself. Just as important, it wouldn't break a window even if the batter was lucky enough to get a piece of it. That simple invention—a lightweight, injection-molded plastic ball with funny holes (the bat came a little later)—made all the difference.

It caught on like gangbusters.

In 1953, the first Wiffle balls went on sale. By the early 1960s, Wiffle was a staple up and down the Eastern seaboard as *the* game to play at picnics, charity events, and school competitions, among others. "Wiffle" quickly became a part of the American vernacular. And not just as a toy that protects windows but as a pastime unto itself.

Why has it been such a success? Part of its charm has to be the simplicity of the idea. Chris Byrne, a.k.a. "The Toy Guy," is one of the toy industry's top consultants. "What makes the toy different, or what makes the toy sustain is that each subsequent generation brings to it their own sense of fun and play," he says. "Things like an Etch-a-Sketch, or a Slinky, or a Wiffle ball, or any of these classic toys, they really are nothing until they are brought to life by the child."

Also—and this is no small consideration—it works. Exactly as advertised, a Wiffle ball curves like crazy, won't break windows, and delivers a satisfying baseball experience. "And, the game, as we know, happens in the imagination, so that the child is imagining that he or she is a big-league baseball player. And the closer it replicates the ability to throw a slider or throw a curveball, or something…that replicates a real baseball experience, you know that's a good toy," says Byrne.

And don't forget that the whole family can play across age and gender lines. Your dad can pitch a no-hitter and so can your sister.

There's the iconic, unmistakable, you'd-know-it-in-the-dark ball. It's old school and new school, unique and ubiquitous. The Wiffle ball remains the great equalizer, as they call it, befuddling batters of all ages. With its humble holes, it curves, zips, and zooms, turning every-one into a major league pitcher. It's a fad-proof fan favorite. Tim Kennedy, president of Kennedy Design, a NYC-based industrial design firm, says there's mom, apple pie, and the Wiffle ball. "I think Wiffle is an American design classic. I would put it in a category with things like the Frisbee, the Airstream trailer, and the Fender Strato-caster, American design products that have just endured as great designs through generations."

Another key to Wiffle's timeless appeal has to be its born-in-the-USA, still-made-in-the-USA pedigree. The same family, the Mullanys, has been making the Wiffle balls for almost 60 years—and still use some of the original machinery.

DID YOU KNOW

The Wiffle ball was originally created from discarded perfume packaging.

Nick Jonas

**Actor; Musician, the Jonas Brothers and Nick Jonas
and the Administration**

. . . On playing Wiffle ball in his backyard in Jersey.

Growing up in Jersey, the backyards are big but not big enough to
play full-out baseball. So finding something to play in the backyard is
always a nice thing. Mine was just big enough, so it was the perfect
Wiffle ball field. All the kids in the area would come over and play.

. . . On what his field looked like.

We had a patio that looked exactly like what an infield would look
like. So we had the patio, and beyond that was a grassy area and
these two large trees that were kind of set up like foul poles. We
would basically play like it was a baseball field, just smaller. And it
worked out perfectly.

　　We would set up the bases and run the bases just like a real baseball game. It usually was about four or five on each team, but it always
depended on how many people would show up. It was a lot of fun.

. . . On his Wiffle skills.

My curveball would have to be my best pitch. Obviously, my fastball
has worked a couple of times. It's kind of fast, I can get it up to 65
or 70 miles per hour on a good day. When we were shooting the TV
show for Disney Channel, we set up a bullpen and would just go out
there every day and throw new pitches. And the pitches were new
and we'd just try to get better.

. . . On his favorite all-time Wiffle ball field.

We've played in parking lots, backyards, and concert venues. Anywhere we can go to get out there in the venues and play is always a
lot of fun. And the arenas especially. They're built like a bowl, so it
works out perfectly for hitting the ball—it's good.

　　The Forum in L.A. [is awesome]. One day, me and a couple friends
set up what we called a "Jonas Olympiad." Basically, it was four
teams and it consisted of Wiffle ball, dodgeball, and then kind
of a thinking game. So, a few different things. But the

Wiffle ball was perfect in the Forum. The seats are kind of rounded in that "bowl." So we set up home plate at the center of the arena [on the old Lakers basketball court] and just hit into the seats. It was amazing.

. . . On who's the best player among the brothers.

My brothers are all right. We all have our moments, but I take it a little more seriously than I think they do. So I would say I'm the best, but we all have fun.

. . . On his favorite Wiffle ball memory.

We were in tour rehearsals in Dallas at the American Airlines Arena, and we set up a game in the parking lot. There was this big wall and it looked basically exactly like a Wiffle ball field, but on gravel. We set up this game, and it started off just for fun and then more people started to join. And it became a nine-inning game. That was probably the best Wiffle ball game I ever played in my life. The score at the end was 6–6, and we ended it with basically a home-run derby. We had to have the two best hitters from each team and two best pitchers come out in a do-or-die type thing. It was a lot of fun. Everyone around us played. My team came out victorious with a walk-off home run by one of the players. It was great.

. . . On his Wiffle ball future.

I think that one day I would love to own a Wiffle ball team. That would be amazing. If I can't play on it, then owning it would be fun. But just the fact that people take it so seriously to me is an amazing thing, because I think that if I had the opportunity to take it that seriously I would.

Today Wiffle ball is bigger than ever. From the Smithsonian to South Park, the white plastic ball has become part of the fabric of American life. Saturday afternoons are for Wiffle ball games, but so are Sunday mornings, and Sunday comics strips have featured Wiffle prominently. Jeffy from *Family Circus* wants to know what happens to all the holes in his "Wiffle (Swiss) cheese." *The Far Side*, *Hagar the Horrible*, and *In The Bleachers*, too, have gotten a kick out of the Wiffle ball.

The Wiffle ball has been enshrined into the permanent collection of the National Baseball Hall of Fame in Cooperstown.

David Eisenhower played Wiffle ball on the White House lawn while his father-in-law, Richard Nixon, governed the nation from the inside.

The Wiffle ball was featured as one of the "Humble Masterpieces" in a recent show by the same name at New York's Museum of Modern Art.

It has been featured in countless advertisements for other products, most recently Target and Converse, providing that essential piece of casual Americana for set decoration.

A Wiffle-themed wedding/ fundraiser in Massachusetts had the 90-year-old grandmother of the bride, Laura Goulet, tossing out the first pitch on her happy day. The scouting report had her as "awesome."

THE FAMILY CIRCUS®   **By Bil Keane**

4-13
Copyright 1988
Cowles Syndicate Inc

"Look. Wiffle cheese."

Even the Beastie Boys have made reference to a Wiffle bat. Enough said.

The Wiffle ball has been enshrined into the permanent collection of the National Baseball Hall of Fame in Cooperstown.

Wiffle seems nearly recession-proof and, even in tough economic times, it continues to sell briskly. How many Wiffle balls have been sold? Only three people know—and they're not talking. A good guess would be in the hundreds of millions, at least.

After nearly 60 years, Wiffle is still a terrific bargain. It costs under five bucks, it's made well, and you can use it again and again. For the price of a couple of slices and a Coke, you've got a full summer of fun.

As new generations of fans continue to discover the Wiffle phe-nomenon, they can thank recent developments like league play and aluminum bats. It's now a whole new ballgame.

To sum up Wiffle's part in the American psyche is someone who gets it: Connecticut governor Jodi Rell. Speaking about having the all-American company in her state's own backyard, she says, "The fact that the maker of an iconic piece of Americana like the Wiffle ball calls Connecticut home is one more feather in our cap. Wiffle ball conjures up so many positive images and emotions. For me, it evokes thoughts of summer, laughter, youth, excitement, family, and fun. Wiffle ball has been, and continues to be, an indelible part of America's recreational pastime."

This is mass-production in practice, this is Bernoulli's Principle and the Magnus Effect in action (more on that later). This is, for crying out loud, what they built the suburbs for. This is Wiffle ball. ⚾

2

History

Edison. Bell. Mullany.

A small list of some of the great American inventors.

Edison's résumé includes the lightbulb, the phonograph, and the motion-picture camera. Bell's?: the telephone. And then there's Mullany. *Who?* Mullany. David N. Mullany, inventor of the Wiffle ball.

The genesis of this iconic product may sound familiar: Hardworking guy makes good and discovers the one-in-a-million idea—but only after trying everything in the book. And make no mistake, the story is a quintessentially American one: A man's love for his family and his love for baseball lead him to invent a new ball for a new game that would spread baseball-inspired fun and bring families closer together all across the country and the world.

You may think you've heard stories like this, but this story is different. This story has a twist *and* a kicker. The twist is, after a string of false starts that often separated him from his family and his need to support them, the guy hits an idea, bringing him closer to his family, *and* giving it a lasting family legacy to pass on for generations.

The *kicker* is, when he hit it, the one-in-a-million idea was literally right in his own backyard.

That man was David Nelson Mullany. He had workingman's blood, just like his dad. He was the lucky one of three Mullany boys to attend college. It was the Depression, times were tough, but David N. left his family's Hatfield, Massachusetts, tobacco farm to strike out on his own. At 18, he headed for the University of Connecticut, where he eventually graduated from its school of business. His father and brothers stayed and worked the family business, growing tobacco for cigar wrappers. Fortunately for the Mullanys, the cigar business was one of the few successful industries during an otherwise bleak economic time.

David N. Mullany was a left-handed pitcher for the 1929 graduating class at the University of Connecticut.

David N. was a decent student at UConn where he doubled as a left-handed pitcher. He graduated in 1929 with his bachelor's degree in business, but couldn't shake the baseball bug.

He moved to Bridgeport, Connecticut, in search of opportunity. Bridgeport was on the rise, and many large companies were prospering there. But while the area's economy might have been growing, Mullany's wallet was not.

While he dreamed of a career as a right-hand man to a corporate executive, Mullany instead found himself as a left-handed starter on a few local companies' Industrial League baseball teams, for which he was paid a small stipend to pitch. These semiprofessional teams were

Jim Bouton

Former New York Yankees All-Star, author of *Ball Four*, and co-creator of Big League Chew

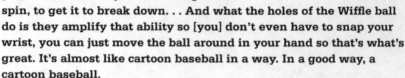

. . . On why every Wiffle ball pitcher is a pro.
A major league baseball requires a tremendous amount of effort and torque on your elbow and on your wrist to get it to spin, to get it to break down. . . And what the holes of the Wiffle ball do is they amplify that ability so [you] don't even have to snap your wrist, you can just move the ball around in your hand so that's what's great. It's almost like cartoon baseball in a way. In a good way, a cartoon baseball.

. . . On Whitey Ford's "Mud Ball."
[In *Ball Four*], I explained how Whitey Ford . . . would wet his hand, spit in the palm of his hand, and rub the ball so there'd be a gob of spit on one side of the ball. At that moment, he would put the ball in his hand and the wet side facing down, and he would reach down and pick up the rosin bag with the ball. Then he would throw the rosin bag down. But the rosin bag was simply a cover for him to get mud on the ball.

So now he's got a ball that's got mud on one side of it. What that does is provide the ball with resistance. And then I use as my example a Wiffle ball. So imagine a big league, major league baseball acting like a Wiffle ball. You have drag on one side of it, just like you have drag on one side of the Wiffle ball that has holes in it.

So if you want the ball to sink, you throw the Wiffle ball sideways with the holes up, and, of course, there's drag and then the ball dives. If you want the ball to sail up, you put the holes on the side, and when you throw it there's drag so the ball will go in whatever direction the holes are. And that's what happened with the mud ball. He would effectively throw a Major League Baseball version of a Wiffle ball.

. . . On loving Wiffle ball.
I loved Wiffle ball because I loved making the ball do something. And since I was already a pitcher, it simply multiplied what I was already able to do with the ball.

comparable to today's lower-level minor league teams. He was playing the game he loved and getting paid for it—sort of.

Mullany was now 24, and holed up the local YMCA in Bridgeport, Connecticut. His fastballs kept him in the game, so to speak, and a string of odd-jobs kept him away from the family farm.

He aspired to secure a job with the local and soon-to-be-infamous pharmaceutical firm McKesson & Robbins (now McKesson Corporation), which produced everything from aspirin to witch hazel.

But as hard as he tried, Mullany couldn't land a gig there. Months went by, and he was staring at a lost cause. He was unemployed, he was broke, and time was not an ally. He had to face the sad realization that heading back to the farm was his surest bet.

Mullany packed his only duffel bag and headed to the State Street bus stop, two blocks from his home at the YMCA.

It was there that fate stepped in, appearing in the unlikely person of a guy named Gus Heskiss. Heskiss was a catcher for an Industrial League rival and worked on the loading dock at McKesson & Robbins. He was on his usual path to work when he ran into Mullany waiting for the bus, and they struck up a conversation. Mullany unloaded his troubles. The next night Mullany was on the mound as the starting pitcher for McKesson & Robbins.

And although no official stats were kept from that game, Mullany did pitch his way onto the company's payroll. The next day, the 24-year old officially entered the workforce on McKesson's loading dock. It was his first full-time job. It was not his dream job, but it was a start for the ambitious young man.

A diligent worker, Mullany proved to be a company man. He was prompt, hard-working, and he never missed a day's work. A month later, Mullany caught an unexpected break. When a superior fell ill, Mullany, a college graduate and good with numbers, was promoted from loading-dock duties to the purchasing department. It was there he got to peek behind the curtains.

Q

What household item was used to make the first Wiffle ball bats?

What he saw wasn't pretty. Executives at the pharmaceutical giant were cooking up a strange brew. They were busy concocting one of the great financial scams of the 20th century. Phillip Musica, company CEO, took over at McKesson in 1925. A former executive at Adelphia Pharmaceutical Manufacturing Company, he used the firm as a front for a bootlegging operation. He was using McKesson's corporate operations to flood the metro area's speakeasies with booze, then illegal under Prohibition.

Musica, a two-time felon, used fake names to hide his identity and acquire control of both Adelphia and McKesson. He hired his three brothers, also under assumed names, to create phony sales documentation and pay sales commissions to Adelphia, the shell company that they controlled, while the moonshine went off of McKesson's docks. Mullany, helping to oversee company inventory, kept his mouth shut. He knew something was stirring, but couldn't figure exactly who or what was involved. It wasn't until later, when the matter came to a head, that Mullany realized it was his bosses who had done the company wrong. Musica was busted in 1938, his double identity was revealed and his bond was revoked. He committed suicide before he was rearrested.

Mullany stayed on for nearly 20 years at the company, all told. When he'd had enough, he and his friend, Zeke Westerson, a recent Yale grad, left to venture out on their own.

David N. Mullany married in 1937 and his first son, David A., was born three years later. David A., now 69, is the keeper of the family history. He recalled the details of his dad's journey over a scotch and burger at the Metro Pub in Shelton, Connecticut.

"After they left McKesson, they manufactured auto polish. It was the first-ever wipe-on/wipe-off auto polish. My dad and his friend, Zeke Westerson, bought the patent for this formulation from the inventor's family. It worked so well and was so easy to use that they started to manufacture and sell it. And they were selling the hell out of it."

Plasticote Auto Polish was a winner, and sales grew quickly. Business was good. So good, in fact, that Mullany and Westerson looked to expand into the South. They hired a New York–based sales agent who began moving product like crazy. Then, strangely, the product started being returned. What they didn't know was that this rep had created a nightmare.

"That sales rep was selling the polish on consignment [without my father's knowledge] and when some of it started to come back, it put the company in a huge cash bind. They also owed taxes. The government said, 'We want our money now!' That forced them into bankruptcy and that was the end of Plasticote Auto Polish," said David A. about his father's successful, yet short-lived business.

Broomstick handles

Things got worse—Mullany had a family to feed. He was in trouble with the taxman and he couldn't get his job back at McKesson. In a short time, the bills mounted. It was 1952. His son, now 12, was oblivious to his father's troubles. So was his mother.

"[Dad] got a job at a fiberglass-cutting operation. He had cashed in his life insurance policy to pay the bills and my mother didn't know it," said Mullany. "He would leave every morning looking for work, and she wasn't aware he didn't have a job. He was in tough shape."

They lived in a modest neighborhood in Fairfield, Connecticut, where houses were built close to one other. There were always plenty of kids around and finding something to do was never a problem.

Young David's childhood was rife with mischief. "People would come into the neighborhood and see all the kids dressed up in World War II garb—flight helmets, goggles, navy pea jackets in the middle of summer, and we'd be chasing one another with BB guns and be shooting one another. It was not safe. For a sidearm, a couple of the wealthy kids in the neighborhood even had pellet pistols. You weren't safe when those guys were around.

"If you got captured, you got tied up and all the buttons were shot off your jacket *while* you were in it. They used you for target practice. That was part of the routine. We had good fun. It was either that or rock fights. You'd be throwing rocks trying to hit your best friend in the head."

He recounts these memories with a sly smile, as if they happened yesterday, fondly discussing his more rambunctious times.

He says his parents told him time and again to find something else to keep him busy. So, like most kids, he ignored them.

It took one last rock fight for the message to sink in. That rock changed the game forever. "I had my hand cocked to throw and somebody I didn't see, someone on my blind side, threw a rock, and they missed my head but hit my rock in my hand. My hand was numb for about two days. Enough was enough."

Thus, the pursuit of more wholesome activities. Like baseball.

"When we first started playing ball, we played hardball at the schoolyard, over at the Grasmere Schoolyard, the neighborhood school in Fairfield, Connecticut. It had a small playground with a backstop. When you hit the ball, it would mostly be off the building or through the windows. So that shot that idea down.

"Then we started using a tennis ball and a sawed-off broom handle. You could sometimes hit the ball onto the roof of the school, but then you'd have to climb up the drainpipe to get it. And then pretty soon, someone would have to call the cops. And the cops said, 'Cut that crap out.'"

Out went the schoolyard, in came a neighbor with a double garage door. So they switched from a hard ball to a tennis ball, but that brought its own issues—tennis balls leave marks. And while that sucker's parents were okay with the marks, Mullany knew it was only a matter of time until they needed to find another place to play.

"I always pulled the ball right onto their stoop," said the lefty. "But the mother was out hanging clothes one day and I pulled a line drive and missed her by an inch, but instead hit the back light. That was it. She kicked us right out of there."

The next set of suckers were the Mullanys themselves. "Yeah, we played at Dave's house," says John L. Belus, a lifelong friend. "That was pretty good, except a couple times we broke some windows."

But that didn't stop the fun at 47 Edge Hill Road in Fairfield, Connecticut, where David A. and friends parked themselves in the backyard of his family's white-shingled house, where the back wall of the house doubled as a backstop. That lasted a few months until shingles dropped off the house.

Exhausted by his son's shenanigans, the elder Mullany kicked the boys out. That left the

DID YOU KNOW

The Wiffle Jr. is identical in size and shape to the original 1953 ball.

younger Mullany, like his unemployed dad, with too much time on his hands. David A. found himself loitering in the neighborhood and rummaging through his house. That's when he found his way into his dad's golf bag in the family garage. In the bag, he found a plastic golf ball. A ball like the ones you'd buy today, it was small and pliable white plastic with circular holes throughout, the holes preventing it from traveling a great distance. Little did he know at the time that the ball would become a source of great inspiration.

David A. and his pals added a sawed-off broom handle for a bat and suddenly found they had themselves a new backyard game. It was a game-changer. "It made it more competitive and you didn't have to chase the damn thing," David A. said. "It was beautiful. You could get away with playing with two guys. It made sense."

That first-ever Wiffle ball field was one for the ages. Belus says there is still nothing like the Mullanys' backyard: "When we played at Dave's house, it was perfect; it had a nice, flat backyard. There was a little brook that ran back down there. If you hit it, one side of the brook and it bounced over, it was single. If you went over the brook, it was a double. If you hit the hill, it was a triple. If you hit it on top of the hill going up to the house, it was a home run. And we ran into the brook a number of times going after the ball. It was a lot of fun."

Fast-forward a year to 1953, and David N. was still unemployed. Remarkably, this was still a secret to his family. The younger Mullany recalls his dad often peeking in at the game but never paying too much attention. He was, after all, scrambling for work. "My dad came home from 'work,' but he still wasn't working… He'd notice us playing hour after hour after hour."

But one particular night in August 1953, the elder's curiosity was piqued.

"What in the hell are you playing?" he asked his son.

"Wiffle ball," he answered.

"What?"

"Wiffle Ball," he repeated. "That's what we call it. When a batter misses a pitch, it's a 'Wiff.'" That was neighborhood slang for striking out.

The senior Mullany was inspired, but that inspiration wasn't without its kinks. "It involved punchin' and fightin'. It would start arguments," recalls David A. "But once we started playing, it had a permanent residence in our backyard. Anybody that had a license to be out of the house would be there."

Mullany Sr. was paying attention. He found himself spending as much time watching his son play Wiffle ball as he did looking for a job. He was smitten with the game.

"He tried to watch me throw a curve with that plastic golf ball. And I couldn't even throw a curve with a baseball. I was inept. My dad was a good left-handed pitcher, and I'm a right-handed pitcher. It never got through to me how to throw a curve. He asked me one day, 'Would it be better one day if you knew how to throw a curve?' I said, 'Of course.'"

The construction of that plastic golf ball made it impossible to throw a curve. The little ball had small circular holes in both hemi-spheres, so when it was thrown, the balanced airflow kept it on a straight plane. So in spite of his efforts, the teenager was left with nothing more than a sore arm.

Years later, in fact, David N. was quoted as saying, "Whether you're playing the outfield or infield, warming up or just throwing the ball around, everyone is trying to throw a curve. Then it hit me, if you could take a plastic ball and make it curve, you'd probably have something."

And both father and son knew it. "Dad said, 'I'll bring home some samples, and let's see if we can get the ball to curve without hav-ing to snap your wrist.'" He reached out to some of his old buddies at McKesson who gave him some plastic parts, half-sphere shapes that were part of a cosmetic package, a plastic gift box for Coty, the perfume company.

The parts were perfect raw material.

"They must've been sample parts they were just kicking around. My dad brought them home and we'd sit there at the kitchen table with razor knives and cutting different designs and gluing them together to make a ball," said David A.

"The finished parts would sit on the table overnight until the glue dried, then I would test them out in the backyard the next morning with my buddy, John Belus, to see if the balls we'd made would work, whether they would curve."

David A. remembers those nights bringing him and his dad close together, even if they did make a terrible mess in the kitchen. It was business as usual for Mrs. Mullany. She was probably more concerned with her mess in the kitchen than the genius at work.

This was the '50s. The term "male bonding" wouldn't have occurred to either of them, but it was obviously a seminal moment for father and son. "What my dad and I had was a mutual operation at that kitchen table."

The Mullanys glued the half-spheres together, creating a light-weight baseball. This in itself did not make a ball that curved. It was their hunch that they needed to create an imbalance in the ball. What began was an exercise in trial and error.

DID YOU KNOW

The Wiffle ball is nine inches in circumference, the exact size of a regulation baseball.

"We even tried gluing a penny on it to put some extra weight in it, but it Mickey-Moused the ball up," says David A.

Cutting into the ball seemed like the next logical step. Armed with a razor blade, they got to work. "We cut and cut to see what worked, and tested its ability to curve," says David A. "It was a lot of guesswork."

"After we got the ball designed it was like, *voila!*"

But on the third night, their luck changed. "This one design looked so nice. It was beautiful.

"It took three nights of screwing around with stuff, and we got it. After we got the ball designed it was like, *voila!* It was like, *Holy* [cow]!"

That design, made at the Mullany's kitchen table on August 14, 1953, is the very design of the Wiffle ball today. And the younger Mullany couldn't wait to get outside with his friends and show it off.

"I'd take the new ball and test it with the guys I played with," Mullany remembers. "I could make it curve, so I knew it was right. We were pretty happy because it was easy to throw and it was bigger and filled our hands up, not like the small little practice golf balls. And we would throw different things with it, curveballs and everything. And we just felt great when we could throw a curveball and have it break two or three feet."

The Mullanys felt the magic in the making. "I told my dad, 'We've got something here. This thing works all the time. You can throw knuckleballs with this, you can throw a straight pitch. It works. And with the plastic ball, you could hit it and it wouldn't damage property. It wouldn't go very far, it wouldn't cost a lot of money to manufacture, and if you could throw a curve, it would be a bonus.'"

They now had a great product in the Wiffle ball, but that wasn't enough.

"He sat me down and asked me what the rules were," David A. remembers. "He said, 'We've got to put this down on paper. We gotta make it right.' He was insistent on getting it right. And they're the same rules today."

Now, finally, they were ready. The Mullany family, with great attention to detail, outlined the first—and final—rules of Wiffle ball. "We wrote them over and over again. I was like, 'Dad, enough already!' But it helped the game. Everybody plays under their own rules but these kept the game competitive yet semi-friendly."

Q What's the total amount of marketing dollars spent by The Wiffle Ball, Inc. since 1975?

Now they were ready to go to market with their idea.

THE RIGHT MAN

David N. Mullany was the right man at the right time to invent the Wiffle ball. He was unemployed and had a strong need to start a business. He had time on his hands and time to tinker and experiment. He had time to spend with his son and he wanted to keep him out of trouble. He had time to observe how much fun his son and his friends could have with a backyard version of baseball and a lightweight plastic ball. He observed that, of all his son's attempts to play backyard ball, the version with the hollow, white plastic ball was the most compelling, not to mention more to a dad's liking as it broke no windows.

Perhaps most important, as a former semi-pro pitcher, he knew baseball, knew it from the inside out. He knew something the casual observer wouldn't know: just how important a curving ball is to the enjoyment of the game.

He even knew the average kid (or suburban dad) would probably hurt his arm trying before learning to throw a backyard curveball. Unless he had a little help.

THE NEXT STEP

So what did an out-of-work car-polish salesman know about making and distributing a plastic baseball and marketing his game? Nothing.

But he was committed to this new project. He scrambled to get institutional financing, but the demise of Plasticote left behind a scar on his financial résumé.

He turned to friends for money and mortgaged his home, which paid his way to a crucial meeting. "We had to get the damn thing made," David A. says. "The people that were already making the plastic golf ball (and, incidentally, the only people anywhere making plastic golf balls) were a company called Cosom from Wayzata, Minnesota. They had a machine shop."

"This guy, 'Clint' Carlson, who owned the company, he was a golfer and made these practice golf balls during the winter. So that's how the plastic golf ball was invented. He had expertise in making molds and had the first patent on how the low-density polyethylene was fused."

THE KEYS TO THE KINGDOM

Mullany recognized that this was how his "Wiffle ball" needed to get made, and he knew Carlson was the guy to help. They entered into a multiyear licensing agreement for Carlson's construction patent and the first-ever mold for the newly created Wiffle ball was developed.

Zero.

The trick was joining the two halves of the ball, sealing polyethylene with heat while keeping the ball soft, pliable, and of high quality. Mullany bought his first plastic

Jeff Griffing
Publisher, *Sports Illustrated*

. . . On growing up in small-town Wisconsin with Wiffle ball.
Growing up in the late '60s and the 1970s, every day, all summer,
all spring, all fall, I'm out with my neighbors, my best friends, my
brother. Every day until the sun's going down, we were playing
Wiffle ball until the fireflies are out at night. My dad's whistling [for
us] to come in for dinner and we're playing until you can't see, and
you're getting hit in the head, and us with our Wiffle ball.

When we'd go to the beach, which was a long car ride away, Wiffle ball always came with us. It wasn't about video games, it wasn't
about television, because there were only four stations at the time.
Everything we did outside somehow involved our Wiffle ball and bat.

I played Little League, Pony League, high school, and I played a
little bit in college. But, it was one of those things that, even when
you were in college, there was always one in my college dorm, there
was always one in my house. It's always been a part of my life.

. . . On comparing Wiffle ball to other sports.
It's like surfing. All you need is waves and surfboard. I don't need to
put gas in it, I don't need to be a member of a club. It's simple. You
have your Wiffle ball and your bat and you make a game out of it.

. . . On what makes Wiffle ball special.
To me, it comes down to the simplicity. You go back to the simple
things. You grab a ball and a bat. No one's getting killed. The genius
of this is that it's pure and portable and it's an extension of America's
favorite pastime, baseball.

sealing machine, which joined the two halves of the ball, from Carlson. It remains a part of Wiffle's factory equipment today.

THE PATENT

If you've ever seen a patent application, you know they're not exactly models of literary light. When David N. Mullany filed an application to patent his "Game Ball" on February 18, 1954, his densely-worded document was no exception. In it, though, if you can wade through the jargon, you will find the precise, scientific keys to Wiffle magic. The description reads:

A game ball comprising a hollow, lightweight, spherical shell, said shell having a substantially imperforate portion, the remainder of the shell having a plurality of closely spaced perforations extending therethrough and providing a perforated zone characterized by surface openings being grouped in one portion of the ball surface to cause the ball to vary unsymmetrically whereby the ball when spinning in flight will follow a curved path.

"Therethrough?" "Unsymmetrically?" Silly? Maybe. Confusing? Perhaps, but it's this patented design that separates the true contender from the army of pretenders. Lots of imitation plastic balls have come and gone, but none of them have curved like a Wiffle ball.

Ironically, Cosom, the very company with the injection-molding machine that helped Wiffle gain entry into a commercial marketplace, even tried selling a ball of its own to compete with the Wiffle ball. The Cosom ball had circular holes all the way around, reminiscent of its original golf ball design. "It failed because it couldn't curve," David A. says.

The copycats should have known better. As anyone who has ever thrown—or tried to hit—a Wiffle ball knows, the unique patented design guarantees that his American original, though often imitated, has never been duplicated.

The patent was granted on January 1, 1957, and the rest is Wiffle history. 👋

DID YOU KNOW ❓

Unlike a baseball, the Wiffle ball can actually rise on its way to the plate.

United States Patent Office

2,776,139
Patented Jan. 1, 1957

1

2,776,139

GAME BALL

William F. Blamey, Jr., Stratford, and David N. Mullany, Fairfield, Conn.

Application February 18, 1954, Serial No. 411,070

10 Claims. (Cl. 273—60)

This invention relates to a ball and more particularly to that type of ball coming within the class known as game or playing balls.

In the playing of games wherein a ball is struck by a bat, or the like, a disadvantage has often been encountered in respect to the limitations of space in certain areas where the game is played. In addition, because of the construction of the ball itself, with which these games are played, injury to property and persons are sustainable. Further, such games are oftentimes not able to be played by younger children or by persons, who, because of the limited space available or for other reasons, do not desire to run in participating in the game. It is therefore desirable to provide a ball of such construction as to be limited in its flight but still having features which would necessitate the use of skill in the use of and play with the same.

It is an object of the present invention to provide a game ball which is so constructed as to be able to withstand great impact and force when struck by a bat or the like without injury to the ball itself.

It is a further object of the present invention to provide a game ball which will not travel any relatively long distance after being struck.

A still further object of the present invention is to provide a ball whose path will vary in flight when thrown and when struck.

A still further object of the present invention is to provide a game ball having all of the aforementioned advantages which is nevertheless inexpensive to manufacture and easy to construct.

Other objects and advantages are set forth in greater detail in the accompanying specification as illustrated by the accompanying drawing in which:

Fig. 1 is a top view of the game ball of the present invention;

Fig. 2 is a side view looking in the direction of the arrow 2 of Fig. 1;

Fig. 3 is a section taken along the lines 3—3 of Fig. 1;

Fig. 4 is a top view of a modified form of the game ball;

Fig. 5 is a top view of another modified form of the game ball; and

Fig. 6 is a top view of still another modified form of the game ball.

In the drawings the game ball 10 comprises a hollow spherical shell 11 of substantially the same size as a standard baseball. While this size is disclosed for the purposes of this description, it will be understood that the ball may be of any suitable size, as for example, the size of a soft ball or the like. The shell 11 is preferably made of plastic material, such as polyethylene or the like for reasons hereinafter set forth, and is molded of the desired shape. The shell 11 is provided with a series of apertures 12. According to the present invention, the apertures 12 do not extend over the entire surface of the ball but instead the ball has an imperforate portion 13. The apertures 12 themselves may be provided for in a

2

number of ways, as for example, by simply cutting them out of the finished ball or within the molding process itself. I have found that the ball having the apertures 12 and the imperforate portion 13 has surfaces of different air resistance and when thrown or struck, will follow a curved path when spinning in flight. The curved path itself can be a very unsteady one, wherein the ball will curve to the right and left and upward and downward during the same flight. Thus, the curving path of the ball when in flight necessitates the exercise of skill to meet the same with means to strike it, as for example a bat or the like. In addition, skill will have to be exercised in catching or fielding the ball after it is struck, for the reason that the differing air-resistant surfaces also cause the ball to curve after it has been struck.

The ball of the present invention will not travel for any relatively long distance despite the force with which it is struck and, in fact, cannot be thrown for any relatively long distances despite the force exerted. As a consequence, there is no necessity for the provision of a large playing area when using this ball and games may be devised with the use of the ball which eliminate the necessity of a great deal of running in connection therewith.

The ball is constructed of a hollow, lightweight, spherical shell and will not cause injury to persons using the same even if they are struck thereby. In addition the construction prohibits damage to property, such as windows or the like, if struck in the area in which the ball is used.

The spherical molded shell 11, comprising the ball, is preferably provided of sufficient thickness so that it may be struck, or strike other objects with great impact without damage to the ball. The material preferably used in the construction of the ball is plastic, such as for example, polyethylene or the like and has structural strength inherent therein. In addition, the preferred location of the apertures in the surface of the ball as hereinafter set forth, eliminates weak spots.

As shown in Fig. 1, the game ball of this invention is preferably so constructed that one-half of its surface presents an imperforate semi-sphere 13. Apertures 12 are provided on the other half of the ball. It is to be noted as shown in the drawing, that the apertures 12 are in staggered relation to each other. This structure adds to the inherent strength of the ball wherein weak spots, which might exist if the apertures were not staggered, are eliminated.

Referring to Figs. 1 and 2, and using as an illustrative example, a ball having a 2¼ inch diameter, it is preferable to begin the row of apertures 14, about ⁹⁄₁₆ of an inch from the equatorial line 15 of the ball. It is also preferable that the apertures be quadrilateral in shape and each ½ inch in length and ¼ inch in width and that eight apertures equidistant from each other be provided in the row of apertures 14 closest to the equatorial line 15 of the ball. In the next outer row of apertures 16, six apertures are provided, also equidistant from each other and of the same width and length as the apertures in the row 14 hereinabove described. In the following outer row of apertures 17, three apertures are provided, also equidistant from each other and the same width and length as the apertures in the row of apertures 14. At the pole of the ball, an aperture 18 is provided which is preferably ⁹⁄₁₆ of an inch in diameter. Each row of apertures is preferably equi-distant from its next adjacent row. While this construction has been described in great detail and results in the most preferable action of the ball with regard to maximum curvature aspects, maximum structural strength and maximum flight potential, it will be understood that other sized apertures may be used in different relationship to each other which

2,776,139

3

would nevertheless provide a ball which will have the features desired as aforesaid.

In the modification shown in Fig. 4, the apertures 14 cover substantially ¾ of the game ball with the remaining ¼ of the ball being imperforate. A ball of this construction may also be used and will follow a curved path when spinning in flight.

In the modification shown in Fig. 5, the apertures 12 only cover ¼ of the surface of the ball with the remaining ¾ of the surface being imperforate. While the ball thus presented does not have the maximum curvature aspects when spinning in flight, it nevertheless may be advantageously used.

In Fig. 6 another modification of the game ball of the present invention is shown in which relatively large apertures 12 are presented on ½ of the surface of the game ball with small apertures 19 on the other surface. It will be understood that the differing air-resistant surfaces provided by the large apertured surface as against the small apertured surface, will also enable this ball to follow a curved path when spinning in flight.

The game ball of the present invention is advantageous in its preferred form and in all its modified forms, in that there is provided a non-injurious, non-damaging ball having structural strength and which will follow a path curving in many directions when spinning and in flight so that the exercise of skill is required in playing the game in which it is used.

While the invention has been described in some detail, it will be understood that variations and modifications may be made without departing from the spirit of the invention or the scope of the appended claims.

We claim:

1. A game ball comprising a hollow, lightweight, spherical shell, said shell having a substantially imperforate portion, the remainder of the shell having a plurality of closely spaced perforations extending therethrough and providing a perforated zone characterized by surface openings, all said perforations and openings being grouped in one portion of the ball surface to cause the wind-resisting characteristics of the surface of the ball to vary unsymmetrically whereby the ball when spinning in flight will follow a curved path.

2. A game ball comprising a hollow, lightweight spherical shell, said shell having an imperforate portion covering at least one-quarter of its surface, the remainder of the shell having a plurality of closely spaced perforations extending therethrough and providing a perforated zone characterized by surface openings, all said perforations and openings being grouped in one portion of the ball surface to cause the wind-resisting characteristics of the surface of the ball to vary unsymmetrically whereby the ball when spinning in flight will follow a curved path.

3. A game ball comprising a hollow, lightweight spherical shell, said shell having an imperforate portion covering at least one-half of its surface, the remainder of the shell having a plurality of closely spaced perforations extending therethrough and providing a perforated zone characterized by surface openings, all said perforations and openings being grouped in one portion of the ball surface to cause the wind-resisting characteristics of the surface of the ball to vary unsymmetrically whereby the ball when spinning in flight will follow a curved path.

4. A game ball comprising a hollow, lightweight

4

spherical shell, said shell having an imperforate portion covering at least three-fourths of its surface, the remainder of the shell having a plurality of closely spaced perforations extending therethrough and providing a perforated zone characterized by surface openings, all said perforations and openings being grouped in one portion of the ball surface to cause the wind-resisting characteristics of the surface of the ball to vary unsymmetrically whereby the ball when spinning in flight will follow a curved path.

5. A game ball comprising a hollow, lightweight spherical shell, said shell having a substantially imperforate portion covering at least one-quarter of its surface, the remainder of the shell having a plurality of closely spaced staggered perforations extending therethrough and providing a perforated zone characterized by surface openings, all said perforations and openings being grouped in one portion of the ball surface to cause the wind-resisting characteristics of the surface of the ball to vary unsymmetrically whereby the ball when spinning in flight will follow a curved path.

6. The invention as defined in claim 5 in which the openings are quadrilateral.

7. A game ball comprising a hollow, lightweight spherical shell, said shell having an imperforate portion covering at least one-half of its surface, the remainder of the shell having three rows of closely spaced perforations extending therethrough and providing a perforated zone characterized by surface openings, all said perforations and openings being grouped in one portion of the ball surface to cause the wind-resisting characteristics of the surface of the ball to vary unsymmetrically whereby the ball when spinning in flight will follow a curved path.

8. The invention as defined in claim 7 in which the row of apertures next adjacent the equator of said shell consists of eight apertures; the next adjacent row of apertures comprise six apertures and the next adjacent row of apertures comprise three apertures.

9. The invention as defined in claim 8 in which an aperture is provided at the pole of the spherical shell.

10. A game ball comprising a hollow, lightweight spherical shell, approximately 2¼ inches in diameter, said shell having an imperforate portion covering at least one-half of its surface on one side of the equator of said shell, the remainder of the shell having closely-spaced rows of closely-spaced quadrilateral perforations extending therethrough and providing a perforated zone characterized by surface openings, all said perforations and openings being grouped in one portion of the ball surface to cause the wind-resisting characteristics of the surface of the ball to vary unsymmetrically, whereby the ball when spinning in flight will follow a curved path, the row of apertures next adjacent the equator being approximately ³⁄₁₆ of an inch from said equator, and each of said apertures being approximately ½ inch long and ¼ inch wide.

References Cited in the file of this patent

UNITED STATES PATENTS

465,507	Windoes	Dec. 22, 1891
837,147	Thomas	Nov. 27, 1906
1,483,165	Eaton	Feb. 12, 1924
1,684,557	Saunders	Sept. 18, 1928
1,873,221	Senn	Aug. 23, 1932

Jan. 1, 1957   W. F. BLAMEY, JR., ET AL   2,776,139

GAME BALL

Filed Feb. 18, 1954

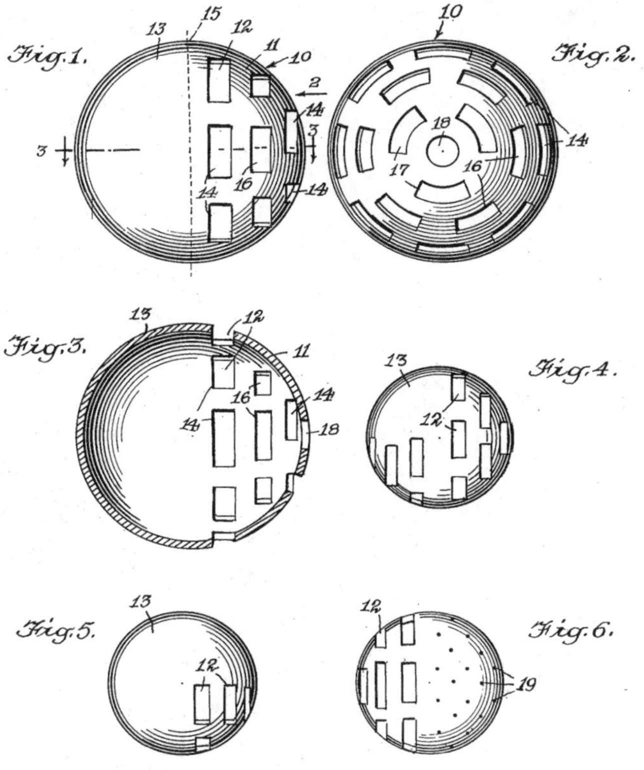

Fig.1.
Fig.2.
Fig.3.
Fig.4.
Fig.5.
Fig.6.

INVENTORS
William F. Blamey Jr
and David N. Mullany
By Sylvester J. Liddy +
Arthur L. Nathanson
ATTORNEYS

35

The Birth of a Wiffle Ball

Colorant and virgin polyethylene are mixed.

Material is sucked into the hopper on top of the injection molder.

The material is fed into a long barrel where it's heated to a molten state.

Plastic is injected into a mold where it takes shape.

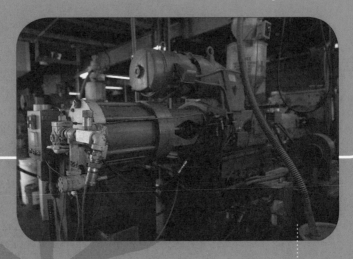

Plastic is then cooled in mold. Ball halves drop out of the mold in preparation for sealing process.

[Note: the slotted and solid half-spheres are produced in separate runs.]

Sealing Process

Halves are separated in an assembly line.

Each half is loaded into sealing head.

A hot plate drops down and heats edges of the halves. Hot plates retract and sealing head closes.

The two ball halves are sealed.

3

The Mullanys:
The Next Generation

Nowadays, David A. Mullany is taking it easier and has passed the baton of the Wiffle Empire to his sons David J. and Stephen. Now in their early forties, the two brothers oversee the day-to-day operations of the company. David J. Mullany is the president of the company and Stephen is vice president.

David J. Mullany is the president of the company and Stephen is vice president.

A trip to Wiffleville—that is, the Shelton, Connecticut, headquarters of The Wiffle Ball, Inc.—is a trip back in time. This unassuming brick building off County Route 8 is the origin of all the Wiffle in the world.

The office is old-school, from the carpet that saw the Nixon administration come and go to the wood paneling that comes from a time when that stuff was actually made of wood. That suits third-generation president David J. Mullany just fine. I sat down with him at his desk and discussed the past, present, and the future of the family business.

David A. Mullany's unmistakable license plate.

The Mullanys hard at work at The Wiffle Ball, Inc.'s headquarters.

What's it like to be at the helm of an American icon?
It's neat. When I take a moment to sit back I think, *Hey, that's pretty cool.* But in the middle of it, I don't always have that luxury. My father worked like a dog and was here at the office all the time. Now Stephen and I are here all the time. It's a nice legacy to have, very nice. It's nice to see what my father and grandfather did and appreciate how they got it from A to B to C.

If your grandfather, David N. Mullany, could have looked into a crystal ball in 1953, could he have ever imagined the phenomenon?
It's kind of against the odds, really. It's not rocket science and we aren't saving the world, but it's a good, fun product. The product is the same as it was then. [That's] what really gives it the staying power.

In 1953, did he think he was biting off more than he could chew?

He thought it was a good idea. He saw value to it. He thought, *If it keeps these kids [my dad and his friends] occupied, if the concept of the game itself kept the kids occupied, then maybe.* Now, if you have the component to be able to throw a curveball, it makes the game that much better. Then he figured, it's going to be worth it.

Your father and grandfather are both competitive guys. Is that what drove them to success?

My dad doesn't back down from anything. Never. That's the way he is. My grandfather was like that to a degree. Maybe it's the Irish in him. Who knows? He was very competitive. *Very* competitive.

Did your grandfather appreciate what he built?

I think he enjoyed it. He liked to see kids having fun with the game or hear that they enjoyed it or how they learned how to hit a curveball playing Wiffle ball. Even today, you'll mention the brand and you'll see folks thinking. Their eyes sort of roll back up to the left, and [they] are like, *Yeah, I remember playing that as a kid.* Everyone always has a fun story about playing Wiffle ball. It's not like you're on a scooter, where everyone remembers when they fell off and broke their wrist.

Does it surprise you that your grandfather was able to pull this off?

He had experience in purchasing [at McKesson]. He had a lot of contacts and knew what stuff cost. So I think he was a pretty good judge of whether he was getting taken or not. He understood the cost of materials and goods and consumables that were necessary, and that's a big part of it. Back then it wasn't like today, where a company can go from virtually zero to king of the heap. That just didn't happen. That was not a function of 1950s industry. Today, you have all the tech stuff. You can go start to finish in a heartbeat now.

My grandfather was not a technical guy, not at all. So to a degree, he had to have a little bit of faith in the guys he chose to handle the manufacturing, machinery, and equipment. He had trusted employees and that made a big difference. He did not have the luxury of being able to do just enough. He couldn't make it just good enough. It had to be perfect.

Wiffle president David J. Mullany

And by "perfect" you mean…?
You start making a crappy product and it's all just going to unravel. In a heartbeat, it can all just unravel.

But your grandfather was a little more of a renegade?
He had to be. I think it's just because he wasn't a farmer. And he knew it. His brothers were. His brothers all stayed up there, went to war.

He would bet on anything. He would bet on two raindrops running down the window to see which hit the bottom first. He wasn't a gambler but he was that competitive.

If there were a ballgame coming up, [it didn't] matter who— Yankees, Red Sox, anybody. He's a Red Sox fan, and you would think he would want to take the Red Sox [but] he'd let you pick [either team]. In my grandfather's drawer there'd always be five bucks [for betting]. At the end of the year, somebody came out five bucks ahead.

It was fun to be around him. He taught us how to play golf. Once we got to the point where we could hit the ball, he'd bet us a dollar. He gave us two shots a hole. And he wouldn't be shy about it. If he beat us, he'd make us pay him the dollar.

Q Why did The Wiffle Ball, Inc. start selling black bats in 1975?

And how did that translate to the business?
In business, you've got to be willing to take your shot. If you win, there's reward. If you lose, you've got to pay. So you better be sure if you're going to make the bet, you better be sure you're not biting more off than you can chew.

Is this your dream job?
Yes, I think so. Like anything else, there are days when you want to slam your head into a wall. I do enjoy it and I really appreciate being in the position I'm in now and doing what I've done for 25 years. I really appreciate what my grandfather and father have done ahead of us. There would be days on end when I wouldn't see my dad because he was always here working. Of course, we knew he was doing it for the family.

You don't actively advertise the brand.
It becomes more complicated. It's a very simple product and very simple business, but the world finds a way to complicate everything.

What kind of Wiffle ball player were you and are you now?
I was decent. I wasn't phenomenal. I hit the ball pretty well, I was a decent pitcher. My best pitch was probably a knuckleball. I had a rising fastball. I could get the ball to rise and then almost stop. I can't do that now. I don't play as I would like to. My daughter, Jill, will give it a go, but I don't think baseball is her thing. My son, David, he's a pretty good player.

Are you surprised at how competitive the game has gotten?
I think it's always been that competitive. Stephen and I played in our own neighborhood and things were fierce. It didn't degrade into brawls like in my dad's neighborhood. It was really competitive, though.

And now that you and your brother are running the company. When did you know, for sure, this would be your career?
You know, it just kind of evolved. When we were little, we'd come in and run the shrink tunnel (packaging machine) on the weekends. We were packing golf balls. That gave us something to do on a weekend. My dad probably didn't want us having rock fights or shooting each other in the face with BB guns like he used to.

Will there be a fourth-generation Mullany running The Wiffle Ball, Inc.?
Who knows? I'll treat it like my folks did. If [my children or Stephen's] want to, good. If they want to do something else, I'd have no problem with it.

In 1975, the OPEC oil embargo made the manufacture too costly to use pure HDPE (high-density polyethylene). Instead, they manufactured bats using reground and repurposed materials, coloring them black to be uniform.

So if they are doing this 25 years from now, what does this office look like?
Probably the same. You know what a hassle it would be to move all this stuff and redo it? Oh my God. I remember the last time we put carpeting in.

The desks are how old?
These are fairly new.

20 years old?
At least. Two desks have been here for a while, probably from the '60s. Another chair here is also from the '60s. There's a spring that's going to goose you. No extra charge. I don't need "stuff" to make me feel good about coming to work. I have a job to do.

I live a pretty simple life, really. Pretty basic. I'm not the smartest guy in the world, that's for sure. I just try to work hard.

What's the best story you've heard from a fan?
How about one that got to me? A detective in New York City wrote me a letter in 2002. He was a NYC cop and he was devastated by 9/11. He described how the one thing that really took his mind away from his grief was playing Wiffle with his son. That was nice to hear. It's the whole element of family, that people enjoy playing it with their family.

What now?
Keep on making them, keep on chunking them out, keep on giving kids a good time. I'm proud of my family. The stuff my dad, grandfather [have] done, it's great. They really did a good job. [They] always make for fun stories. My dad, his stories are wild. Even my grandfather, he always had good stories.

Stephen Mullany and I sit on a workbench inside the Wiffle factory just after lunch. He just spent about an hour tweaking a loose wire on the Cosomatic.

Family businesses are often difficult. You guys seem to have a unique rhythm.
To be honest with you, it's the way my parents brought us up. They always said, 'It's you and your brother.' And, even when we were little, my friends would fight and hit each other with baseball bats—for real. But we've always stuck together. I guess that's probably why it's been easy to work together. Why waste your time fighting and arguing over nonsense when you could use your time more wisely making Wiffle balls? I guess we're lucky.

You handle more of the things in the factory while your brother runs the operations.
I was never really a big office guy. I enjoy doing mechanical stuff. We both do a bit of each.

What was it like working with your grandfather?
It was great just to be around him. He was the nicest guy, and I'm not just saying that because he was my grandfather. He was unique.

DID YOU KNOW
Wiffle balls were first sold at a diner in Woodbridge, Connecticut.

He created a product that was a stroke of genius without even knowing it. That's often how the great companies are built.
And he was not a mechanical kind of guy. All the stars were lined up right, and it just worked out. Some people have the knack to be in the right place at the right time, and I guess he was one of them.

What is that special magic attached to the Wiffle brand?
I think it's just because people have such a good time with it as kids. As they got older they had fun with it, too, but now you're bringing your siblings in, your kids, everyone. I, myself, love it. I go home and I pitch to my son, Stephen, and my daughter, Jessica. I have a box of balls at home. And they'll stand there and swing as hard as they can until I stop throwing. I get a kick out of it.

Does it mean something different to you that this is your brand that you're throwing?
Yeah. As I get older, now that I have kids, I think that I appreciate it even more because I can play with them. And it's like, *Oh, this is pretty neat, playing with something that my grandfather and my father invented*. Not many other people can say that. It's pretty neat.

You were at a wedding recently and had a brush with fame.
Ha! I'm walking down the aisle, and I hear, "Oh, that's one of *them*." And I'm thinking, *I know where this is going*. And you could tell they wanted to ask. The guy was probably in his mid-sixties...it was neat, and you do get a lot of that. But, I mean, the people that I'm friends with, they couldn't care less.

Talk about the fan mail.
We get stuff from grandparents. We get stuff from kids who can barely write and we have to try to decipher what it is they're saying.

That's kind of neat, you know? And they draw the pictures of [themselves] playing. It's interesting.

How has the product changed in nearly 60 years?
We've been doing it the same way from Day One. We've never fudged the quality my grandfather started.

Wiffle vice president Stephen Mullany

You and your brother Dave played a lot as kids. What's your favorite Wiffle memory?
Some company came out with a pitching machine [that was used for Wiffle balls] and it would shoot the balls out. I'd say I had to be 12 years old. And you couldn't make it pitch as fast as we wanted, so we had to get closer to the machine. Now we're like 10 feet away. My brother lets one go from the machine, and I just swung. I didn't think I was going to hit it because it was going fast and I was so close to the machine but—*bam!*—I hit it 150 miles per hour. I hit a line drive right off Dave's head. And he's running around, "I'm blind! I'm blind!" It was just ridiculous, if you could have seen him run around.

DID YOU KNOW
The Wiffle ball was invented by an unemployed auto-polish salesman.

Tell me about the bats. They're made off-site. How does the process differ to that of the way the balls are made?

The bats are blow-molded [Wiffle balls are injection-molded]. Air is blown into a mold that forces the plastic to the outsides of it, the same way a water bottle is made, for example. A mold closes around the parison [a white wax]. And, then it blows air into the middle of it and it forces all the plastic to the outsides of the mold and it's cooled and that's why it's formed.

That's a whole different process than the balls, it's more like a 24-hour process. We did do it for a while, but it got to be a pain. My grandfather had a molding company, B&D Molding, which is right up the road. It got to be too much, so they got out of it.

If anybody can make a plastic mold, if the process is so ubiquitous, what makes the Wiffle ball so special?

It's the idea behind it I guess. That's gotta be it.

Are "Wiffle" and "Mullany" synonymous?

Oh, by all means. I mean, that's what we have, our name. Really.

Are people surprised when they learn about how modest this operation really is?

Oh, yeah. We have truck drivers that go cross-country and they stop here and they're like, 'Is this the world headquarters? This must be something else.' People tend to think it's this huge company. It's a big name, but it's a small company. We've got 10 to 12 people here in total. It's always been that way.

What will Wiffle be like in 30 years?

That's a good question. I don't really see it being any different. I mean, it's worked for this long. You can't reinvent the wheel, so what more do you need?

What happens if your kids work here? Will they ask for mahogany desks? Top-of-the-line computers? New machinery?

Ha! We do the same thing at our house. What we have we maintain. It's not like we just throw stuff out. What we have we've had for a long time. When my kids screw up something with my house I'm like, "I've had that since I was little."

WIFFLE THROUGH THE YEARS

1953–1955
The Wiffle ball goes on sale for $.49. The Wiffle Ball, Inc. offers fans free official Wiffle ball rules.

1956
First bat and ball set are released. Retailing for $2, it's clamshell-packed with one Wiffle ball and a generic 32" (ash) broom handle, 1 1/8" in diameter, called "The Wiffle King."

Images of Boston Red Sox Ted Williams and Jackie Jenson and New York Yankee Whitey Ford are licensed for use on packaging.

1957
Regulation baseball–sized Wiffle ball released.

1958
Milwaukee Brave Ed Mathews joins Jenson and Ford on Wiffle packaging.

1959 –1960

Wiffle Bouncer Ball, Wiffle Basketball, Kick Baseball, Football, Wiffle Stik Ball, Wiffle Tot-Balls and Wiffle Golf Set are introduced. Stik•Balls have perforations in both hemispheres of the ball.

Wiffle Basketballs and Kick Baseballs created using blow-molding technology.

Basketball and Kick Baseball are phased out after two years. Wiffle Kick Football never makes it to market.

1961

Wiffle introduces their familiar yellow plastic bats to complement wooden "Wiffle King" bats. The bat is 30" long and 1¼" inches in diameter.

The Wiffle Paddy Wacker released. It resembles a cricket paddle but is marketed as a "safe, gentle persuader." It sells for just under $2.

55

1962

Wiffle's famous "header sleeve" packaging, modeled after the Chinese finger trick, goes on sale. It was conceived at a Warner Packaging Christmas party.

Header sleeve doubles as "Wiffle Toss," a one-man hitting game that allows the batter to toss the ball up in the air to himself before swinging. Touted as "a Revolutionary New Idea in Batting Practice."

Two-dozen Wiffle floor display is introduced.

1963-1965

Bat and Ball-O-Matic Set, a one-player batting game goes on sale. It is sold with a Wiffle ball, bat, and kickstand. Phased out after three years.

1966-1974

Wiffle discontinues sale of wooden Wiffle King.

Flying Saucer and Flying Scaler introduced.

1975

Black, not yellow, plastic bats are sold during the OPEC oil embargo .

1976

Embargo now longer in effect, yellow bats go back on sale. A new textured treatment on bat handle replaces grip tape.

1977

Short-lived Wiffoam Ball released marketed in response to Parker Brothers' popular Nerf ball.

1978–1979

Wiffle Sports Spectacular Collectors Series is released under license with the Major League Baseball Player's Association The set included one circular pog-like trading card with every boxed ball, featuring 188 players including:

1. Lee May/Baltimore Orioles
2. Bert Blyleven/Pittsburgh Pirates
3. Richie Zisk/Texas Rangers
4. Vida Blue/San Francisco Giants
5. Jorge Orta/Chicago White Sox
6. John Montefusco/San Francisco Giants
7. Tony Perez/Montreal Expos
8. Wayne Garland/Cleveland Indians
9. Frank Tanana/California Angels
10. Randy Moffitt /San Francisco Giants
11. Garry Maddox/Philadelphia Phillies
12. Ted Simmons/St. Louis Cardinals
13. Gene Tenace/San Diego Padres
14. Buddy Bell/Cleveland Indians
15. Willie Stargell/Pittsburgh Pirates

1981

Strike 'm Out set, including pitcher's rubber and home plate, introduced. Also introduced was Hit and Run! set, which consisted of pitcher's rubber and home plate, plus first, second, and third bases.

2009

The Wiffle Ball, Inc. trademarks the color yellow for ALL plastic baseball bats.

Today

Current catalog includes Junior, Baseball, and, Softball—sized Wiffle balls, sold individually and together with bats; 24" Junior-size Wiffle bat; solid (unperforated) baseball and softball Wiffle balls; Flying Saucer; Scaler; and Wiffle Golf Balls.

4
Leagues

So there I was in Yale Hospital, my ankle wrapped tighter than King Tut.

I didn't need no stinkin' X-ray to tell me I'd torn my Achilles, you just know. I told the cute nurse I hurt myself lion-taming, but she wasn't buying it. "Wiffle ball," I finally confessed.

It was a delightful Saturday afternoon in New Haven, and I was basking in the glare of fluorescent lights with metal crutches being shoved up under my armpits. Delightful.

Organized, scored, statted, paid, and yes, professional Wiffle ball is a phenomenon—a fast-growing, swervy, curvy phenomenon at that.

Lion-taming, Wiffle ball, it's all the same. I'd just been carried off the mound an hour earlier, pitching relief for Team Wicked Cow in my first-ever competitive Wiffle ball tournament.

It was the bottom of the first when it all unraveled—never a good sign. That's when I was called in as a left-handed reliever. My buddy, Chris, was getting shelled like I'd never seen any pitcher get shelled before. *Bam! Bam! Bam! Bam!* One shot after another sailed over the fence.

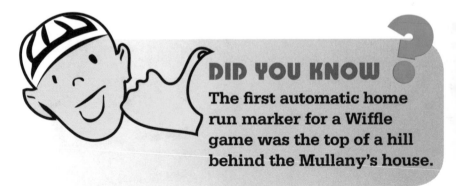

DID YOU KNOW

The first automatic home run marker for a Wiffle game was the top of a hill behind the Mullany's house.

My colleague Perrie, our outfielder, frankly spent more of her time retrieving our gopher balls than anything else. It was obvious we were way, way out of our league.

In Chris' defense, he was once a wannabe pitcher for UCLA—and our would-be ace—but it was his first competitive Wiffle experience, too, so we cut him a break. In the two minutes or so that I spent in relief, things didn't go much better for me—or my Achilles.

Pop.

Back to delightful. The hour before the chaos, and before our first game, the three of us spent time taking BP and eating donuts. So did the other 50 guys there.

Like Trix, I thought Wiffle ball was for kids. Not exactly. These guys were serious. It was pretty chill and lot of these guys already seemed to know one another. Each three-person team had plunked down a hundred bucks for a chance to win a thousand in the day-long tournament. Some had even traveled over three hours for that chance. It was 10:00 AM on Saturday in a sleepy Connecticut town. What were these guys doing?

We soon found out. As we sat on our coolers and beach chairs, game time approached. And here were players busting out hockey tape, meticulously wrapping up the handles of their yellow Wiffle ball

DID YOU KNOW

And the first single marker was over the brook behind the Mullany's house.

bats. Some were doing jumping jacks and others were running wind sprints. Wind sprints, for God's sake.

This is Wiffle ball, right?

Most came out in uniforms with clever team names screen-printed in the front and a funny Wiffle-related nickname on the back. Of course, everybody had a uniform number.

As the game began, and my buddy Chris was getting shellacked, one thought burned, *This ain't your mama's backyard*.

Welcome to the world of organized Wiffle ball. Hell, welcome to the world of professional Wiffle ball. Yup, I said it, professional Wiffle ball. If that seems like an oxymoron to you, you need to read this chapter and see what you've been missing. Organized, scored, statted, paid, and yes, *professional* Wiffle ball is a phenomenon—a fast-growing, swervy, curvy phenomenon at that.

Guys with uniforms, guys with fields, with leagues, with stats, with trades, with tournaments, with championships, guys with big brass Wiffle balls, coast-to-coast—these guys mean business. Just how many people spend their time in organized Wiffle competitions is still a matter of conjecture, but it's safe to say that about 50,000-strong would be a good place to start.

Who are these guys and how did this happen? When did Wiffle ball become a sport? What's a professional Wiffle ball player? And where is this phenomenon headed?

The Wiffle ball—famous for its zips and zoops—now had a new element attached to the summer game: heat. The newish breed of player brought to Wiffle another fundamental connection to baseball—the fastball. And these are no ordinary fastballs. We're talking fastballs with speeds that equal that of a major leaguer's—high 80s, low 90s.

Add to that a three-foot break and you have a batter who's in for some serious trouble.

Gary Dell'Abate a.k.a. "Baba Booey"

Executive Producer,
The Howard Stern Show

. . . On playing Wiffle ball through the years.

I always played Wiffle ball as a kid. Even as you got older, I remember my buddies and I would get together when we were in our thirties with our families.

. . . On a local and well-publicized Wiffle ball controversy.

An interesting thing happened last year in my town in [Greenwich] Connecticut. There was an abandoned piece of property in between a couple of houses that belonged to the town but wasn't being used. And a bunch of kids got together and turned it into a small Wiffle ball field. They put up a Green Monster. It was really bare-bones, but it was fun. And before you know it, all the kids wanted to play Wiffle ball. It was really awesome. I went down there one day with my kids and my kids ended up playing.

I just kept being drawn to the field because it was so old-fashioned and sweet. Just one of those things in a hustle-bustle world.

[Author's note: Pressure from neighbors then forced authorities to close the field to play.]

. . . On the appeal of the game.

With baseball, my kids don't say, "Hey, get a bat and ball and meet me at the field," because they're all so busy playing baseball in a more organized fashion. And after that thing went down and I have a fairly big front lawn and [it's] flat, the kids would play Wiffle ball here. They got a big piece of wood in the back for their home run wall. I really found that enjoyable, that it sort of sparked them.

My dog loved it, too. We wound up buying three-packs of Wiffle balls because my dog kept eating them every time they'd go over the fence.

Let's take a deeper look at how the competitive game got started and how, from it, these leagues and tournaments have evolved. There are thousands of organized Wiffle events every year. We'll define an event as a league, a tournament, or a charity event. Impromptu backyard Wiffle games don't count here; only those where there is an "organizer" and a sign-up process, per se.

From this, legendary teams and players have emerged, and in the process, the game has changed. We'll look at five people, five true believers, who made the greatest difference in how the modern game is played.

RICK FERROLI

To find the "Godfather" of organized Wiffle ball, we hearken back to 1970s, and to Boston, where a local chap named Rick Ferroli, as legend has it, was the first guy to give birth to a competitive Wiffle ball tournament. This big dream began for this city kid in the 1960s. Ferroli fondly recalls the three constants from the family front porch: concrete, cars, and windows. Or, in other words, Wiffleville. He grew up playing a lot of Wiffle ball and turned out to be a decent baseball player, even spending a spring training with the Phillies as a 23-year-old. In between, he'd

DID YOU KNOW

Wiffle ball bats are yellow "because that was the color of every baseball bat in every comic strip at the time," says David A. Mullany.

played high school ball in the Boston suburb of Hanover. When he came to grips with the hard reality that his pro dreams were just that, he set out to trade one major league fantasy for another.

"How about if I turn your backyard into a miniature Fenway Park?" Ferroli suggested.

"So what did we do?," Ferroli said. "We played more Wiffle ball." With a combination of "passion, money, and time," he says, Ferroli parlayed his love of the game into the next-best thing: beating the stuffing out of people by playing Wiffle ball. Those competitive juices still flowed and Ferroli knew he was good.

When he was in his late-twenties, Ferroli and his friends organized a series of round-robin Wiffle ball tournaments in his neighborhood. The "season" consisted of 10 games, and players threw down 50 bucks a head. The winning team took the pot.

It was a breakthrough. Ferroli instantly knew he was on to something. That simple premise of pay-for-play begat his next idea: building a big-time Wiffle Stadium. And with an assist from his mom, Ferroli wasted no time.

After a death in the family, the then-twentysomething Ferroli had moved back in with his mother. He had an idea for a project that would take both of their minds off their grief. "How about if I turn your backyard into a miniature Fenway Park?" Ferroli suggested. Her reply: "Knock yourself out."

With some hard work, just months later Ferroli had a reasonable facsimile of Fenway Park, "Apollo Field," as he called it. It even had its own Green Monster.

Build it and they will come. Ferroli's goal was to expand the competitive game from Boston's South Shore to neighboring states and eventually to draw teams from other regions. *We gotta get some publicity so we have more competition and see just how good we are*, he thought. So he did.

The local media were immediately smitten with the new field: *The Boston Globe* and *The Boston Herald* coverage of the newly minted Apollo Field helped turn the place into a national curiosity. "From that day on," Ferroli says, "my life was never the same."

The field, creation of a formal governing body, and an official rulebook—are the legacy of Rick Ferroli.

By day, Ferroli owned a contracting and commercial cleaning company. But now, this Bostonian was Pope-like. "I'm sitting down to dinner and the doorbell rings. It's a family from Iowa. I mean a family—mother, father, three or four kids. And they say to me, 'We just wanted to touch the field. We just wanna touch you.' I'm like, *Oh, my good God. Here we go.*"

So what made Saturdays at the Apollo such a curiosity?

"Right in my mom's backyard, I built the Green Monster and I put in an electronic scoreboard. I had a screened porch that was for the VIPs. I made a little diamond and put pegs in where you could see your men on base because we didn't have base runners. I put distance markers on the outfield fences (100 feet to dead center, 85 to right, and 66 to left). I put in 300-watt halogen lights, seven light towers for the night games (which maxed out his mom's electricity). Then I found a guy looking to move a full-size Citgo sign (the real Fenway Park has one) from a gas station. Of course, I had to go and take it. Then I mounted it on the roof of my mother's house."

That's what.

A real ballpark just seems to suggest a real league, doesn't it? Perhaps a group or an association at least. Ferroli took his plan to another level, this time creating an entity, a governing body to oversee play at Apollo Field. He called it the World Wiffle Ball Association.

In that inaugural year of 1987, the WWBA signed up 32 two-person teams at $75 a pop. That double-elimination tournament was still, at least in some sense, in his mom's backyard, so Ferroli's first consideration was to be respectful. Filling 200 slots would've been no problem, he said. A year later, he found himself drawing teams from 20 states—and those teams meant business. Many of them had hardcore baseball pedigrees.

As important as the creation of Apollo Field and the WWBA are, Ferroli's key contribution to modern-day competitive Wiffle ball is something even more important: his 47-rule rulebook. Ferroli recognized, just as father and son Mullany had three-and-a-half decades earlier, the importance of clearly outlining the rules on paper. He printed *The Official Rules of the World Wiffle Ball Association*, the first known rules of what is effectively competitive Wiffle ball.

"I spent a lot of time making the rulebook. And it was revised, I think, probably three or four times based on the growth that it took over a three-year stretch. I needed to make it more enjoyable [in order] for more people to participate. A two-man game became obsolete quickly."

Ferroli's rulebook served as the bible for many future organized Wiffle ball leagues and tournaments.

The first tournament rules stipulated:

- The angle created from the tip of home plate will be 90 degrees from foul line to foul line.
- Seven innings equal a normal game.
- All championship games will be nine innings.
- No base running.
- 48 feet from the mound to home plate.
- Three-ball/two-strike counts.
- A ball may be scuffed up between innings only.

Why these rules? Why 48 feet?

Here's the organized Wiffle vision Ferroli saw at the time. Players were getting better. The biggest concern of this new competitive style was that games were becoming too advantageous for pitchers.

In his time, Ferroli had regularly witnessed pitchers throwing upwards of 70 to 80 miles per hour, leaving the hitter very little chance at the standard 42-foot pitching distance. Ferroli knew that the rules needed to be adjusted accordingly. His new rulebook, in part, was created to help balance the pitching and hitting segments of the game. It was a small but seminal move to push the mound back six feet, but one that got the ball rolling.

"[The game] became pitching-dominated. Once that happened, the offense was taken out of the game. It became 1–0 games into extra innings, then no score into extra innings. It just seemed to be unfortunate."

The 48-foot distance gave batters a crucial few extra milliseconds to see the ball.

These three things—the field, creation of a formal governing body, and an official rulebook—are the legacy of Rick Ferroli. In 1991 he traded in professional Wiffle ball for fatherhood, and the WWBA retired on top. Although Apollo Field is a distant memory, Ferroli had made his mark and laid the groundwork for many serious Wifflers to follow.

MIKE ALESSI

Mike Alessi, like Ferroli, saw the Wiffle train coming from miles away. But unlike Ferroli, Alessi regrets, he didn't have a yard big enough in which to build a mini Fenway Park. Still, Alessi will tell you he's satisfied with his contribution to the game.

It was back in 1986 when he launched his first eight-team Wiffle ball tournament, the Fall Ball Classic, in Stratford, Connecticut. He recalls spending days handwriting promotional posters which he posted in local stores and delis. It got him the attention he needed.

Grady Sizemore

Cleveland Indians Center Fielder;
Three-time All-Star; Two-Time Gold
Glove Winner

. . . On growing up playing Wiffle ball.

I remember playing in my backyard. My house had a big pool in the middle of the backyard and it caused so much destruction. It was one of those things that got in the way of every Wiffle ball game and caused a lot of controversy. And, here we are, all these little kids arguing over the most simple of games in the backyard, fighting over every out and every run.

It was a free-for-all. We ran the bases, and I remember getting pegged with a Wiffle ball when I was off the base, which was an out. Guys were getting hit in the face. It was an all-out war.

. . . On whether he still plays Wiffle ball.

I still play in my backyard. Home-run derbies . . . I still grab a Wiffle ball every now and then.

[The great thing about] Wiffle ball is that you can build your own field. You always seem to make parts of your backyard turn into walls, fences, and guidelines that aren't really there. In our yard, if you can get it on the roof, that's a homer. But if you can get it over the roof and onto the street, you get bonus points. If you knock it into the pool you get [negative] points, if you knock it into the hot tub you get double [negative] points.

. . . On whether his all-star baseball skills translate to Wiffle ball.

You would think so, but I'm not going to say I've won every game. Wiffle ball is tough because it doesn't always play out the way you want it to. Put a perfect swing on there, and you still get screwed.

Little did he know he was adding another element to the new world of competitive Wiffle ball: guerrilla marketing.

Though you could hardly say he generated a big buzz, Alessi would call it more of a soft hum.

But he was out doing it—hustling, getting the word out, using the local media as no one else in the Wiffle ball space had done. Little did he know he was adding another element to the new world of competitive Wiffle ball: guerrilla marketing. Remember, those were the pre-Internet days, so it was hard enough to determine the viability of building a tournament-based business, much less trying to hook teams to drop some dough to play. But Alessi was creative in his approach and he built a solid product that he first called the Stratford Wiffle Ball Association.

His great challenge was that leagues and tournaments simply didn't exist at the time; he was navigating uncharted waters. He was staking everything on the belief that his love of the game of Wiffle ball was shared by others and that folks would spend money to play. His vision was to pull players out of their backyards and into more centralized, competitive environments. He bet right.

By spring 1987, just six months after his initial trial run, the tournament participation more than tripled, to 25. That fall, the number jumped to 42. For the next decade, Alessi produced two tournaments annually, Fall Ball and Spring Fest.

Then the floodgates opened. In 1996, Alessi created a regional, multi-state tour called Wiffle Up!, the first of its kind. Tournaments were held in Long Island, Philadelphia, Cleveland, St. Louis, Pittsburgh, and Providence, among other locales.

These tournaments now draw an average of 50 teams each and as many as 127 teams, says Alessi. The tournaments are broken down into two brackets: fast-pitch and medium-pitch.

It was obvious that Alessi had found the Wiffle holy grail: a way to get people playing the game and make money doing it. He got folks to build teams. He got would-be players to play. That was no easy feat—especially back in the day.

"I love sports so much. Wiffle ball tournaments, for me, have always been unique. I'm one of those guys who never quits. If I dedicated my time to it full-time it could be a big business. I have a proven commodity [in Wiffle Up!]."

Now, almost 25 years later, Alessi's still doing his thing. Only now, his Wiffle Up! tournaments span nine states, with 16 tournaments each summer. He has a database chock full of current and prospective players totaling more than 7,500.

"It's a cult," said Alessi. "I've known guys who put Wiffle before their marriage and it's caused a lot of problems." Spoken like a true fan.

MIKE PALINCZAR

Next in line is "the Czar of Wiffle ball," as he's known: Mike Palinczar. He's a star on the mound *and* behind the desk.

A police officer from Trenton, New Jersey, he created his own series of Wiffle tournaments under his organization, the New Jersey Wiffle Ball Association. Now in its 20th year, the NJWA thrives as one of the country's largest tournament circuits, with more than

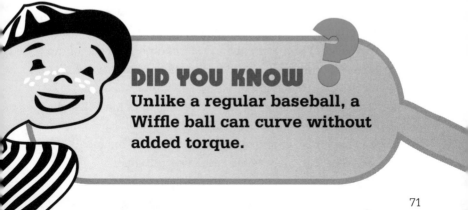

DID YOU KNOW
Unlike a regular baseball, a Wiffle ball can curve without added torque.

NJWA founder Mike Palinczar, making a Wiffle Pro bat.

100 teams of three to five players, from the spring through the fall season. He guesses that since its inception he's seen more than 1,000 different teams in his tournaments.

Palinczar's coup is that he's still on top of his game. On one side, he's "the Czar," a force on the field. On the other, he's the owner of one of the best Wiffle ball–based businesses around, managing the NJWA, its tournaments, and its multi-thousand-person database.

In addition to playing Ferroli's tournament, the other big turning point for Palinczar—as it is with many "Wiffle league commissioners," as they're called—was figuring out the Internet and how to use its ability to market the games in and out of his area. NJWA's website, www.wiffleballusa.com, went live in 1995 and became one of the first websites on Wiffle ball outside of its official site, www.wiffle. com, which is owned and operated by The Wiffle Ball, Inc.

It was in 1997, through Palinczar's website, that Major League Baseball got wind of what was possible. MLB executives approached Palinczar to help them organize their first-ever MLB-branded Wiffle tournament. The first one was held in Cleveland, Ohio.

The Mullanys and The Wiffle Ball, Inc. were not involved, but Palinczar and the MLB pushed on, calling their initiative "Yardball." Yardball lasted from 1998 to 2000 before it sputtered. It's a legitimate question whether or not its failure is attributable to their inability to use the name "Wiffle."

Another Palinczar contribution to competitive Wiffle ball—and it was a biggie—was the creation of the first officially licensed aluminum Wiffle bat, the aluminum Wiffle Pro Black Magic.

With competitive pitchers throwing the Wiffle ball more than 75 miles per hour, it became apparent the yellow bat was not heavy enough to stand up against such speeds. Palinczar, keeping it in the Wiffle family, secured the Mullanys' blessing to design a bat for the professional leagues. The Wiffle Pro is sold at Palinczar's tournaments, in addition to NJWA-branded plastic bat alternatives.

After years of investing thousands of dollars into organizing tournaments over the years, Palinczar says that at about $100 a team per tournament, he's finally starting to turn a small profit. But that's not why he does it.

"I do it for the love of the game," says Palinczar. And while organizing tournaments is what takes up most of his time these days, he is still a competitive player at heart. "The hard part is, for me, [that] I run these tournaments, but I also play. So while I'm mowing these guys down and talking trash, I have to be nice to them too, because I want them to play in my tournament."

LOU LEVESQUE

Because of the efforts of Lou Levesque, the game can truly be said to have gone pro. It was Levesque, with his creation of Golden Stick Wiffle Ball, who brought in the idea of licensing multiple versions of the same brand-name teams—the Risers, the Bombers, the Diablos, the Snipers, among others—and branding them across multiple regions of the country. Levesque's innovation, a true regional league, combines some of the fun of fantasy sports leagues with the actual knuckles-on-the-ball excitement of real professional sports. There are uniforms, logos, stats, trades. There is also publicity. There are even "salaries."

The advent of his GSWB has had an indelible impact on the sport of competitive Wiffle ball and on the people who play it. "We are really tapping into the pro player inside of everybody," says Levesque.

Levesque, 33, currently works in insurance in Hamilton, Massachusetts. He started his league, Golden Stick Wiffle Ball, in 2002. He has been playing Wiffle recreationally "forever," since his childhood in Salem, Massachusetts.

He would be the first to admit that he backed into his Big Idea. "I was always the one in the neighborhood to take things to the next level. You couldn't even play hide-and-seek in my neighborhood without me keeping stats. Every single thing we ever did. So that kind of spilled over into my adult life."

His game-related ventures didn't often pan out well. "I ran a Madden tournament on XBOX. Failed. I ran a mini lacrosse tournament. Failed. I just wasn't giving my all. A couple of guys who were [involved] in the first two failures told me I couldn't get a Wiffle tournament done, that I was all talk."

Apparently, that was all it took. His first tournament was a Sunday morning of June 2002, and by midafternoon, he believed he'd struck gold: "I turned to my partner and said I was going to turn this into a league."

He created "franchises": 32 teams for which he devised names and logos, which he relicensed (that is, sold) to local and regional directors, who would, in turn, do the same in their own locales. "I had guys coming in and paying me to be a team…that I assigned to them. I can't even believe that I pulled that off."

Levesque had struck a chord deep in the Weekend Wiffle Warrior psyche. "I think that the reason these guys choose Wiffle ball is the fact that they can just get two or three people and have a team,

"We are really tapping into the pro player inside of everybody," says Levesque.

GSWL president Lou Levesque

whether it be [to] enter a league or just play together."

So what does that mean to be a professional player in Wiffle ball? "To be recognized, to be discussed, to have a bad game, to be talked about, and to have a good game, to be celebrated. It's very image-driven."

Recognition is all very nice, but what about those "salaries?" Does being a professional Wiffle ball player mean getting paid? Sort of and not really. You have to win.

Golden Stick does not pay actual salaries to its players. Rather, it has a "Salary Point" system, a system that rates players' values. By Golden Stick's rules, a team can only have so many players with a certain number of points, a salary cap, of sorts. It helps level the playing field by forcing teams to distribute their points amongst their players.

Being a pro *can* mean real money. GSWB's national championship purse is, on average, $10,000 each year. That is serious stuff.

Does the "professionalization" of Wiffle ball put some Wiffle lovers off? Perhaps. Levesque remembers, "When the salary system came out, for instance, people were saying, 'This is just Wiffle ball. Why can't we just play?' Nobody wanted to take away [from] the purity of the game. People didn't want to graduate to the next level. They wanted to keep it just pure. I think that in my league people find the perfect balance between the purity and the format because it still is the game, it still is Wiffle ball.

"This is not your backyard. In your backyard, you're not going to be facing New York for Game 3 of the national championship for five grand. So, if you want to play in your backyard, that's great. That's the essence of the game. But if you want to take it to the next level, call me."

BILL OWENS

Bill Owens, like many of today's competitive Wiffle ball players, had his 15 minutes of baseball fame at the college level. He spent much of the 1990s traveling around the country competing in Wiffle ball tournaments. By 2001, Owens kicked it up a notch, founding arguably the most competitive Wiffle organization yet: Fast Plastic.

A self-described "tournament-league," Fast Plastic today has 11 regions across the country from Long Island to Los Angeles and St. Louis to Boston. Here's how it works: Each region hosts three tournaments leading up to one national championship in Austin, Texas. The prize for the winning team is $10,000. Unlike GSWB, pre-registration is not required; a player or team can show up on the day of a regional tournament and compete for a seat in the national championship.

Fast Plastic is generally regarded as the most serious and cutthroat of the Wiffle competitions. Keep in mind, none of these leagues or tournaments are mutually exclusive. A member of a GSWL team can play a Wiffle Up! tournament or a Fast Plastic regional qualifier. In fact, in 2009, an overwhelming majority of the top teams at Fast Plastic's National Tournament were GSWL players.

The East Coast/West Coast, Golden Stick/Fast Plastic rivalry should not be ignored. There's a lot on the line as both heavyweights wrangle for the top spot in big-time Wiffle ball. GSWL may have the professional league structure, but Fast Plastic has tournaments coast-to-coast. Only time will tell which organization will rule them all.

Along with these five difference-makers, each of whom has made a significant contribution the Wiffle cause, there are others who have benefited the game in ways that should be acknowledged.

ROB PIERVINANZI

Organized Wiffle ball, just like organized baseball, has superstar players. One such Wiffleballer who dominates any contemporary discussion of the sport is Rob Piervinanzi. "Wiffman," as he's known, works in mobile communications by day and by night serves as the New York Regional Director for Golden Stick, arguably the fastest-growing and most significant professional Wiffle league. Clean-cut and well-spoken, he's poised to become an avatar of this game.

A Queens native, baseball is in his blood. His dad was a profes-sional ballplayer who was drafted by the Boston Red Sox. Piervinanzi's Wiffle ball pitching has been called "extraordinary"; he regularly hit a jaw-dropping 90-plus mph on the radar gun in his prime. ("Prime" for Wiffle ball pitchers often ranges from 19 to 25 years old.)

"I was in my prime at 19, I was throwing as hard as anybody. With drops." Today, Piervinanzi, at 25, throws 75 to 80 miles per hour. "It's a drastic drop, but 75 with a Wiffle ball is still fast. People are like 'Wow, how do you hit that?' And I'm like, 'Please, if I threw that to anybody who plays in a league, it's gone.'"

Asked which is harder to hit, a 70-mph Wiffle ball or a 90-mph baseball, his answer is unequivocal. "A Wiffle ball, no question."

Piervinanzi approaches his craft with the seriousness and discipline of a big-leaguer. "I play three or four times a week. I pitch. I have a schedule to make sure my arm stays in shape. I have

Rob "Wiffman" Piervinanzi swings for the fences.

workouts. I swim once a week for shoulder workouts." To practice, he throws 40 to 50 pitches a day. "As much as it takes to get it right. It's all muscle memory. It's all your release points on every single pitch."

His dedication and insight have paid off. At 23 years old, Piervinanzi and his teammate, Zack Riccobono, spent spring and summer 2009 winning nine tournaments and pocketing $10,000.

In his first year in Golden Stick, he and his team, the Revolvers, advanced to the national tournament. They ultimately lost in the third round.

Beyond his playing fame, Wiffman has become an advocate for the organized game. His gig as GSWB's New York State regional director includes overseeing the growth of the league in the Tri-State Area—New York, New Jersey, and Wiffle ball's own home state, Connecticut. He's putting in his time.

"Golden Stick is eight weeks, three games every Sunday. Series, playoffs, semifinals, regional championship. [Basically] just like baseball's regular season."

What attracts him to the organized game? "I love the competitiveness. The [simplicity]. It's a plastic ball, a plastic bat that you drive all the way across the country for. It's incredible."

Asked which is harder to hit, a 70-mph Wiffle ball or a 90-mph baseball, his answer was unequivocal. "A Wiffle ball, no question."

DOOM

Another renowned player of the game is Wiffle ball all-star Adam Trotta. Trotta, 36, along with Kevin Ostertog, also 36, head up arguably the best team in the game, DOOM. This team has the lifespan of a feline, 17 years and still going. Suffice it to say, such longevity is extremely rare in the world of competitive Wiffle ball. After 106 championships, they remain on top of the game.

DOOM was born in answer to a local flyer for a Massachusetts-based Wiffle ball tournament, one that is still run by Jeff Hammond and these days known as "Wiffle Rock." The team was created nearly two decades ago, it's been nonstop Wiffle tournaments

Adam Trotta of DOOM, Wiffle Ball's most heralded team.

"THE BATTING STANCE GUY"

He answers to many names: George A. Ryness IV or "Gar" (his real name), "the guy with the least marketable skill in America" (his name for himself), or, as he's known to many, the Batting Stance Guy.

Batting Stance Guy is the Wiffle ball player's wildest dream. With the remarkable ability to emulate the nuances of the batting routines of thousands of current and former league baseball players, you can say the 36-year-old has a skill like none other.

He's been showcased on Letterman, ESPN, in several boardrooms and in several major league ballparks. For the Batting Stance Guy, he's living the dream.

The Batting Stance Guy as Brian Giles.

When did this bizarre hobby start?
When I was seven with those wooden novelty bats and the five-dollar helmets I would get at Giants and A's games.

What was your first imitation?
Pete Rose. I got him in my first pack of baseball cards. But my Jack Clark [impression] was really the first to make my friends laugh.

How at seven years old did you learn those nuances?
A lot of *This Week In Baseball*. A lot studying baseball cards.

Who has the best batting stance in the game today?
Kevin Youkilis, because he takes elements of all the best stances. And how can you have your bat pointed more to the pitcher than Julio Franco? He has his hands separated and [the bat is] pointed and he's bouncing and his knees are together. How do you top that? And all the profuse sweating.

What level of fame does an MLB player have to attain to be imitated?
Zero.

What's the best reaction you've gotten from an MLB player?
Mike Cameron of the Brewers. He was rolling around and couldn't stop laughing. He was screaming he was laughing so loud.

Has any player not liked what he saw?
I definitely had an awkward interaction with Josh Beckett. He comes over and says, "You do pitchers?" So I say no, but I do players' reactions to pitchers. I can do [Angels catcher] Mike Napoli against you in the [2008] playoffs [after he homered twice]. Nothing. Crickets. Beckett was not into it. And he was like, "Do you have a day job? You should keep it." This is an MVP of the World Series telling me I'm a loser. He's right.

Who's your favorite to emulate?
Ben Oglivie, Gary Matthews Sr., and Moises Alou.

Who has the best nuance?
Gary Matthews Sr. He's got the Brian Downing thing going on, open stance, then closed, then shimmying back and forth. And when he hits it. He'll get rid of the bat downward and then jump and straighten his arms as if he can't believe he just touched that thing it's so hot. And the way he'll start dancing. It's unbelievable.

You are who every Wiffle ball player wants to grow up to be.
That is not lost on me. This whole year, interacting with the [MLB] players, really on my own terms, in shorts and a T-shirt, whatever I would wear in the backyard playing Wiffle ball, baseball and Wiffle ball have been good to me and I want to love them back. Seriously, there's enough snarky websites out there, they've got that covered. I like the idea of keeping it *Andy Griffith*-light. Fun, with a touch of nostalgia. That's what I feel good about.

The Batting Stance Guy does his best Moises Alou.

ever since. The team plays together nearly every weekend, tournament or not.

He may be older than a lot of gunslingers, but Trotta's still bringing it as one of the best fastballers around. But these days, he leaves much of the pitching to the younger players on his team.

Like any good GM, Adam has built his team by combining youth, talent, and chemistry. DOOM has found that mix in twentysomething rising stars Dallas Mall and Troy Parks.

"There has to be some sort of chemistry there. So luckily for us, Adam has gotten the right type of guys [who], for whatever reason, the chemistry is right," says Mall. Really? Chemistry in Wiffle ball? "It's a game of 'catch fire,' but then you also get real cold. We've got to be balanced. We've got to be able to depend on each other."

DOOM's nearly two-decade run has brought unprecedented success. Trotta estimates upward of $60,000 in winnings.

But for Trotta, the best is yet to come.

"We would like to be treated like any other major sport. We're not there yet. We've been paying a lot of money over the years to play and if there was ever a market for it, how cool would it be to get paid to play?"

Other Wiffle legends include Pat Leahy, Josh Pagano, Gary Lavoie, Joe Love, Joe Nord, Tom Locascio, Ryan Wood, Joel Deroche, and Jim Balian.

Other top teams: In the Box, K9s, Rookies (also sometimes known as the Phenoms), and the A Brothers.

DID YOU KNOW

DOOM has won more than 100 competitive Wiffle ball championships.

YARDBALL

Brett Bevelacqua is a filmmaker and editor in Rockland County, New York. Bevelacqua makes a good part of his living editing commercials and programs for major television networks, but it wasn't until a casual pickup Wiffle ball game a few years back that he had a vision of his own: making a documentary about Wiffle ball. And he did just that. *YardBall* (not to be confused with MLB's failed enterprise) is a unique look at the world of professional Wiffle ball leagues. The hour-long piece was a labor of love, as he spent more than 35 weekends over 15 months producing the film.

He admits that he didn't know what he was in for. "I didn't think people would take the game so far. The biggest shock was that people would travel 1,500 miles to play Wiffle ball."

The documentary aired on syndicated cable and inspired Brett to create his own 80-team (and growing) Wiffle league, the Palisades Wiffle Ball League. "As much as making a film, playing Wiffle ball, for me, is just a release from everyday life."

HOW TO GET IN THE GAME

Want to get in a game? It shouldn't be too hard. Wiffle ball games come in all shapes and sizes and, of course, all skill levels. The Internet is Wiffle's new best friend. As it has been for most affinity-driven activities, the Internet Age has helped join disparate Wiffle fans together and has helped grow and organize the community by leaps and bounds.

From Facebook to MySpace to Meetup, fans have chosen social-networking tools to find games. Searching "Wiffle ball" on Facebook will yield more than 500 results for Wiffle ball groups nationwide. The same MySpace search will return more than 4,000. Sites like Yahoo! Groups and Craigslist provide no shortage.

It is also as simple as Googling "Wiffle ball" + your city. [See the directory at the end of this book for a Wiffle ball league near you.]

Recreational sports leagues have also been quick to add Wiffle to their menu of offerings. ZogSports a large recreational league in New York and New Jersey, includes Wiffle ball in its offerings.

Organized Wiffle ball games can also be found on most college campuses, at local rec centers, at summer camps, and at community fundraisers. In fact, Wiffle ball for charity is no joke. You rarely see charities rallying folks around badminton or soccer fundraising efforts, but Wiffle ball seems to have found a unique home with professional charities as a go-to fundraising activity. In fact, several Major League Baseball teams have used Wiffle ball in their charitable efforts. The nonprofit arm of the Cincinnati Reds, the Reds Community Fund, organizes an annual Wiffle ball tournament to raise money to renovate Cincinnati-area baseball fields. Charlie Frank, executive director of the organization, is blown away by the response. "The number of folks that play competitive Wiffle ball has been staggering to us. We had teams in from Arizona, the Carolinas, from Tennessee. It's unbelievable."

DAVE RINGLER

Most people might not appreciate being called a "fat bastard," but Dave Ringler of Grand Rapids, Michigan, would tell you it's a compliment. Every August, he and his fellow "Fatties" put together a one-of-a-kind charity Wiffle tournament. The three-day extravaganza draws teams from up to 14 states and three countries. Is it the Woodstock of Wiffle ball? "There's a big campfire. People are camping here, tenting here. There's at least a couple of hundred spectators for our championship game," says Ringler, King of the Fatties and founder of Fat Bastard Wiffle Ball. The $115-per-team entry fee brings in about $4,000 each year to a local charity.

Muggsy Bogues

14-year NBA star. At 5'3", he is still
the NBA's shortest player.

. . . On why Wiffle ball was instrumental to his NBA success.
That's where it all started with the hand-eye coordination. I was in
the rec center in Baltimore, Maryland, and every morning, part of
our sessions was playing Wiffle ball. And that plastic bat and that
ball with the holes in it, trying to make contact, and I was probably
only one-foot tall at the time! As I get older, I can see now where that
hand-eye coordination came in and the timing. It was from playing
Wiffle ball.

And the Wiffle ball, at that age, just trying to concentrate so
heartily with that long stick in my hand, I had to choke up just to hold
a hit. When you miss, you just hear the wind. And that's something
you don't want to keep hearing.

. . . On his first Wiffle ball home run.
At our rec center, the Wiffle ball field was only about 10 feet long, but
at the time I probably thought it was 100 yards. Like Yankee Stadium,
we had this wall. The top part was white and lower part was blue,
and it was a home run if you hit that white part. I had to get enough
power to hit it at the wall. So I had to stay back on my right leg and
get my power. As soon as that little Wiffle ball came and I hit my first
home run, I felt like I was king of the world.

The Wiffle ball on vacation with Dave Ringler.

Ringler has also taken Wiffle on the road. His favorite travel companion—a Wiffle ball, naturally—has ridden shotgun to far-flung places including Brazil, Germany, and Stonehenge. He even pulled an *I Love Lucy* with a British Bobby. "I held the Wiffle ball up to him to take the picture, and the guy started chuckling. And I kind of looked at him and said, 'Hey, buddy have you ever seen one of these before?' And he kind of out of the corner of his mouth says, 'Yes.'"

5

How-To

Now that you have a sense of Wiffle's history, the product through the years, and its place in our popular culture, it's high time we share the top secrets on what it takes to play like a pro.

If you simplify the game of baseball, being good often comes down to two things: pitching and hitting. Same with Wiffle ball. Of course, we understand the importance of base running, fielding, and overall game sense, but fundamentally: *no pitch, no hit, no game*.

In this chapter, I'll speak to the stars of the game to learn what sets them apart. I'll review pitching and hitting, the rules of the game—and the paradoxical rule that there are no rules. I'll describe the pitches—how to throw a curveball, a screwball, a knuckleball—and how to hit them. explain how taping a bat and scuffing a ball can elevate a player's game. And I'll describe how to start a Wiffle ball league.

Mike Palinczar, founder of the New Jersey Wiffle Ball Association and longtime pro standout Rob "Wiffman" Piervinanzi, New York Regional Director of Golden Stick Wiffle Ball League and currently one of competitive Wiffle ball's stars, dispense helpful hints and reveal their secrets for becoming world-class Wifflers. It's top-secret stuff, highly confidential information.

DID YOU KNOW

Some competitive Wiffle ball pitchers have been clocked at more than 90 miles per hour.

HOW TO PITCH

Former New York Yankee great Jim Bouton told me there's one surefire quality that makes a great pitcher: "Having the courage to challenge the hitters." I expected nothing less from someone nick-named "the Bulldog." But that's the great thing about a Wiffle ball—it comes standard with built-in courage. What exactly does that mean? It means you can be confident as a pitcher when you're not going up there throwing meatballs, because the ball naturally curves. So long as you can locate your pitch, you'll get some natural break on the ball. It puts the onus on the hitter.

Of course, in Wiffle ball, the trick is to keep the batter guessing. By keeping the ball as hidden as possible during the windup and release, changing speeds, and moving the ball around the strike zone, there can be a lot of variation in pitches.

Rob Piervinanzi, who's been known to top 85 miles per hour with a Wiffle ball, says any pro pitcher worth his weight has the following seven pitches in his repertoire: the straight fastball, the curve, the screwball, the riser, the sinker, the knuckleball, and the change-up.

The trick, he says—and what any good baseball pitcher would do—is to mix up the pitches (speed, location, and type of pitch). Another insider tip: The easiest way to change speeds with any pitch, Piervinanzi says, is to throw the ball, any pitch, by putting a finger in one of the holes. This will put significant drag on the pitch while allowing the pitcher to maintain arm speed and angle.

Piervinanzi's special pitch is his "sliser" (slider/riser). The pitch is thrown straight over the shoulder, aimed at the left knee of a right-handed batter (thrown from a right-handed pitcher) and finishing up and away. It's filthy stuff—ask any batter who's faced him.

The invention of new pitches in Wiffle ball is limitless. No two pitches will break in exactly the same way. In changing arm angles and grips, you are sure to come up with a pitch that you can call your own. The only way to learn to throw your own version of these pitches is to practice using several arm angles. Practice, practice, practice.

Consider the following tips from both Piervinanzi and Palinczar, each of whom have been known to throw a Wiffle ball in the high 80s. Master these, and you too can be a star. Note: Success rates and mileage may vary.

THE STRAIGHT FASTBALL

What it does:
One of the easiest pitches to locate, it has little to no break.

How to do it:
1. Grip the ball so holes face the plate.
2. Place index and middle fingers over the top of the holes of the ball, ring and pinky off to the side of the ball, and place your thumb over the bottom seam of the ball.
3. Release with an overhand or three-quarter arm motion.

THE CURVE

What it does:
Breaks in the opposite direction of the curve and slider.

How to do it:
1. Grip loosely, with holes "in," or toward the body.
2. Place index finger along the seam of the ball, middle finger spread two inches from the index finger, thumb on the seam of the ball, and ring and pinky fingers are together against the center of the ball.
3. Release with an overhand motion, with a quick snap of the wrist on release.

THE SCREWBALL

What it does:

Breaks from right to left for right-handed pitchers and from left to right for lefties.

How to do it:

1. Grip loosely, with the ball holes "out," or away from the body.
2. Place middle finger slightly to the left of the  holes, index finger spread two inches from the middle finger, the thumb on the bottom of the ball along the seam and in the middle of the two fingers. Pinky and ring fingers are held together against the center of the ball.
3. Release with an overhand motion, with a quick snap of the wrist at release.

THE RISER

What it does:

Rises as it goes.

How to do it:

1. Grip the ball with the holes facing down.
2. Hold index and middle fingers tightly together above the holes and along the seam, thumb and pinky together touching the center of the ball.
3. Release sidearm with a whipping motion.

Hint from the Pros: Bending the knees helps lower the release point of the pitch so it can rise into the strike zone.

THE SINKER (a.k.a. THE DROP)

What it does:

Breaks lower as it goes; bottom drops as it nears the plate.

How to do it:

1. Grip with holes facing up.
2. Place middle finger and index finger together on the side of the ball. thumb on the seam of the ball, and ring finger and pinky together, touching the solid part of the ball.
3. Can be released anywhere between three-quarters-arm and side-arm.

Hint from the Pros: To throw the drop pitch most effectively, reach toward the plate as far as possible at release.)

THE KNUCKLEBALL

What it does:

"Dances," oscillating back and forth.

How to do it:

1. Grip tightly, with holes facing the plate.
2. Dig fingernails of the index finger and middle finger into the seam, place thumb on bottom seam of the ball, and ring and pinky fingers together.
3. Release overhand, pushing out the index and middle finger toward home plate, holding a stiff wrist at release.

THE CHANGE-UP (a.k.a THE OFF-SPEED PITCH)

What it does:

Allows a pitcher to change speeds but use similar arm angles and release points.

How to do it:

1. Can be thrown as a variation of any pitch.
2. Grip the ball using any standard grip.
3. Place index finger into the closest hole.

Golden Stick pitchers know how to throw a change-up: index finger into the closest hole.

SCUFFING THE BALL

If you want a little edge, keep reading. In baseball, these tips will get you ejected; in Wiffle ball, they'll make you a hero.

Think of them like learning how to throw a spitball. Only a little less disgusting.

Scuffing and knifing are the black arts of Wiffle ball. For pitchers looking for a little more bite on their curveball, here's how to do it.

Piervinanzi says both scuffing and knifing create turbulence around the ball (see also: Magnus Effect), giving the ball extra break and making it travel less predictably. He claims he's seen as much as twice the break in his pitches when the ball is scuffed properly.

The following tips come straight from Piervinanzi, the master of the scuff.

SCUFFING

1. Rub the slotted side of the ball with fine sandpaper until rough. Any hard surface also works, e.g., concrete, asphalt, or dirt (especially black dirt or sand).
2. Rub the ball back and forth on the surface until you achieve the texture that feels comfortable to grip the ball. (Be careful, Fast Plastic league rules state clearly the ball cannot be scuffed/cracked deeper than one-quarter inch.)

KNIFING

Provides a more consistent and predictable surface than scuffing.

1. Using a serrated knife, cut the ball in eight even slices (like a pizza), navigating through the holes and all the way around the ball.

2. Cut Xs in between the spots, and three Xs in between the slots.
3. Knife around the "equator," the seam of the Wiffle ball.

OTHER METHODS

1. According to mdwiffle.net, a blog dedicated to the history of competitive Wiffle ball, dented balls are another option. According to the site, a knuckleball is said to have more movement when the ball is slightly dented so that the index, middle, and ring finger can be placed in the dent. This makes the "push-out" more pronounced, giving the ball more movement.
2. Zack Tawatari, a right-hander for New York University's baseball team and avid Wiffler, says taping the ball is another way to give a pitch some life. Adding tape weights the ball, allowing it to be thrown harder. Taping asymmetrically will also generate spin toward the weighted area. Unevenly distributing the weight (via tape) will cause the ball to move end over end, producing more movement on the pitch.

HOW TO HIT

Who out there in Wiffle-land has not fantasized about standing in the batter's box as their favorite major leaguer? I'm certainly guilty of it. Mickey Rivers was my guy. "Mick the Quick" would twirl that bat after every foul ball better than any majorette. Me, too. Being a solid Wiffle ball hitter requires many of the same skills needed in hitting a baseball. Be comfortable and balanced in the batter's box, see the ball, have quick hands. Piervinanzi, also a one-time college ballplayer, says being a good Wiffle ball hitter is all about bat control. You hit with your hands because the Wiffle ball will travel no more than 125 feet. Having a quick bat and achieving solid ball contact, he says, is favored over a long swing.

HOW TO WEIGHT THE BAT

There are also a few tricks to give the bat a little more pop. These improvements are meant specifically for competitive leagues; the yellow bat is meant to suit the vast majority of players.

STUFFING/CORKING

Piervinanzi says that stuffing a bat—which he does not do—is a fine line. Weighting a bat makes it heavier, which, he says, can slow down a hitter's bat speed. But Palinczar says the stuffing the bat adds "spring" to the point of contact, which may help the ball go farther. Following is his suggested method:

1. Cut the knob of the bat off with a construction blade, using the diameter as an outline.
2. Stuff the bat with desired materials. Styrofoam, the experts say, seems to work best to maintain bat speed, while still adding weight. Newspapers, socks, and hand towels are commonly used.
3. Tape the knob carefully back onto the bat.

TAPING

Simply put, taping the bat adds weight. And, the more weight in the bat, the greater the force of the bat. Piervinanzi recommends the following method:

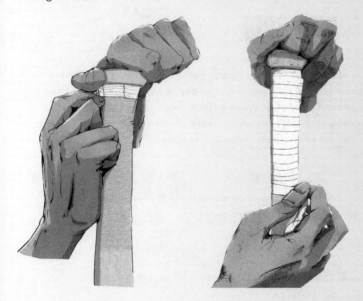

1. Place the bat in your nondominant hand while sitting, with the bat between your legs.
2. Place the tape—cloth, electrical, or hockey tape all work—in your dominant hand.
3. Place the tape parallel to and directly adjacent to the knob.
4. Pull and twirl the bat (like a hockey stick), slanting the tape the higher you go on the bat, and cover desired area of the bat.

Some batters fancy taping the bat on the sweet spot (the middle of the barrel) with hockey tape. It helps create a "whip" through the hitting zone and can also give the hitter a little more zip.

KEEPING SCORE

Keeping accurate score is as important in Wiffle ball as it is in any other competitive sport. Each Wiffle game, league, tournament has its own set of house rules. Ensure that the rules are clear to both sides before beginning play. To avoid barroom-like Wiffle-brawls, please also consult the chart below to determine each party's responsibility:

	Batter	Fielders
Official scorekeeping	🎳	🎳
Fair and foul calls	🎳	
The line calls: single, double, triple		🎳*
Check swings	🎳	
Determining if "tag" was yelled soon enough or loud enough		🎳

* Made by the fielder closest to the ball.

HOW TO START YOUR OWN LEAGUE OR TOURNAMENT

Of course, this may not be as simple as 1-2-3… but below are some simple steps to consider, courtesy of eHow.com:

1. Estimate the number of players you think will join your league.
2. Advertise the league in your area newspaper.
3. Pick a location, like a large backyard or empty field that can be marked off with something as simple as spray paint or cones.
4. Plan out a schedule.
5. Know the rules. The rules and variations that exist in Wiffle ball are different from Major League Baseball.

Palinczar agrees that advertising is the key to starting a league or tournament. Social networking sites like Facebook, MySpace, Twitter are great tools for getting the word out.

Of course, the folks at Wiffle recommend league organizers contact them for all the proper use of the Wiffle name and brand.

For more information on Standards for Certification, visit Wiffle.com.

12. The Association will not use the Wiffle trademarks on merchandise without written authorization from The Wiffle Ball, Inc.

13. This certification does not create a partnership or joint venture between the parties and neither party shall have any power to obligate or bind the other.

14. The Association shall act hereunder as an independent contractor and shall not be deemed expressly or by implication to be an agent, employee or servant of The Wiffle Ball, Inc. for any purpose whatsoever.

15. The Association shall comply with all applicable state, federal and local laws in connection with the Tournament and sale of goods bearing the Certification Mark and The Wiffle Ball, Inc. shall not be responsible for the consequences or any violation thereof. The Association shall be responsible for all duties, tariffs, taxes, reports, fees and other similar charges or requirements imposed with respect to the sale by the Association of the Goods sold under the Certification Mark.

16. Any dispute relating to these standards or this agreement will be litigated in Connecticut and not elsewhere, and the association agrees to Co

I,_____
[ASSOCIATION]

By_____
Name:_____
Title:_____
Address:_____
_____

Please sign and mail this docum
for your records.

STANDARDS FOR CERTIFICATION
BY THE WIFFLE BALL, INC.

1. WIFFLE® perforated plastic balls must be used exclusively in all tournament games.

2. The Certification Mark "Sanctioned WIFFLE® Tournament" will always appear in the following form and font. (The certification mark may not be altered or modified.)

3. The Association may use the certification mark on all advertising and promotional material including, but not limited to, league/team posters, print and online advertisements and schedules. All material must be approved by The Wiffle Ball, Inc. prior to its first use.

4. During any game sponsored by the Association, there shall be no sale of alcoholic beverages, no sales of tobacco products, no drug use no foul language, no inappropriate behavior or clothing which may in any way demean or denigrate The Wiffle Ball, Inc. or its products.

5. The certification mark cannot be used in conjunction with any advertising of alcohol, tobacco, drugs or prurient material.

6. Any violation of these standards shall result in the immediate termination of permission to use the certification mark or other WIFFLE® trademarks in connection with the event.

7. The Association shall indemnify and hold The Wiffle Ball, Inc. harmless from and against any and all claims of third parties and damage, suits, liabilities, losses, costs and expenses, including reasonable attorney's fees, arising by reason of or in connection with the tournament. The Association will defend or settle any matter relating to liability for personal or property injury.

8. The Association shall be fully responsible for and agrees to pay the cost of all investigation, defense, legal fees and payment for any settlements or judgments resulting from any complaint, demand, claim or legal action encompassed by the foregoing indemnity provided that Association is notified promptly in writing of any such complaint, demand, claim, or legal action.

9. The Wiffle Ball, Inc. will control any matter relative to the validity, enforceability or scope of the certification mark "Sanctioned WIFFLE® Tournament" and/or any of its trademarks and trademark registrations.

10. The Wiffle Ball, Inc. will retain ownership and control over the Certification Mark and all marks featuring the term WIFFLE used in conjunction with the event.

11. The Association will not seek to register as a trademark or domain name the word WIFFLE, alone or in combination with any other term, without a written license.

275 BRIDGEPORT AVENUE
P. O. BOX 193
SHELTON, CT 06484-0193

Dear Wiffle® Ball Enthusiast,

Thank you for choosing one of America's favorite backyard games – Wiffle® ball. Three generations of our family have dedicated themselves to the company, and of course to you, our valued customer. We thought we'd take a moment to tell you a little about ourselves, and how the game of Wiffle® ball originated.

It all began when our Grandfather was watching our Dad (who was 12 years old at the time) and a friend play a game, in their backyard in Fairfield, Connecticut, using a perforated plastic golf ball and broomstick handle. They had given up on baseball and softball – not enough players for two teams, not enough space for a field and too many broken windows.

After days of trying to throw curves and sliders with the golf ball, dad told gramp that his arm felt "like jelly". Gramp had been a semi-pro pitcher and knew that throwing curveballs was not good for young arms and thought he might be able to help. He got some plastic parts from a nearby factory, cut out various designs and sent dad out to test them. They both agreed that the ball with eight oblong perforations worked the best. That's how the Wiffle® perforated plastic ball was invented. To this day, we don't know why it works . . . it just does!!

The ball was easy to curve and harder to hit, with lots of strike-outs. In our Dad's neighborhood, a strike-out was called a "wiff", which led to our Brand Name and Registered Trademark "WIFFLE". The rules on the back side of this page were based on the rules that dad used in his backyard games. When gramp saw how much dad and his friends enjoyed the game, he thought that others would too. A year later, in 1953, the first Wiffle® perforated plastic balls were produced and sold. The game caught on pretty fast and now the balls are available in many countries around the world.

From our family to yours, we hope that you enjoy many fun-filled hours playing Wiffle.® We have always tried to produce the highest quality product at an affordable price. We feel that we have done a good job over the more than 50 years of making Wiffle® products and are doing everything possible to ensure that we'll be here for at least another 50, so your children's children can enjoy a good game of Wiffle®ball.

We thank you again for your patronage, and hope you will continue to enjoy Wiffle® perforated plastic balls and bats in your games.

Very truly yours,

David J. and Stephen A. Mullany
THE WIFFLE BALL, INC.

P. S. Please do remember that all plastic bats and balls are not the same. Look for the WIFFLE® brand – the trademark that will assure you of high quality, durable, most playable equipment for your games.

Straight from their backyard in Fairfield, Connecticut, here are the official rules of Wiffle ball.

WIFFLE*BALL
JUNIOR, BASEBALL AND SOFTBALL SIZE

THE BALL—

The Wiffle® Ball was designed to take the place of baseball, stick ball and soft ball for boys and girls in back yards and city streets. It is made of a tough rubbery plastic – is light in weight and cannot be thrown or hit any great distance. The Wiffle® Ball is also an excellent indoor ball.

THE CURVE—

The Wiffle® Ball is thrown like a baseball and will curve very easily. The drawings below show how the ball should be held for curving and controlling the ball.

CURVE	STRAIGHT	SLIDER

To throw the ball straight – and this is important – the Wiffle® Ball should be held as shown.

THE GAME—PLAYED WITH THE WIFFLE® BALL

As stated above the Wiffle® Ball was designed for use in congested areas. Because the ball will not travel far when solidly hit, ball chasing and base running have been eliminated. An ordinary broom handle can be used as a bat if a Wiffle® Bat is not available. The size of the playing field is optional, but we recommend a minimum dimension 20 feet (8 paces) by approximately 60 feet long (25 paces). The field is laid out with foul lines and markers for single, double, triple and home run areas. See sketch of suggested playing field.

The minimum number of players required to play a game with the Wiffle® Ball are two – the pitcher and batter – one player to a side. The maximum number of players that can compete are ten – five players to a side. If a full team is playing, each side will consist of catcher, pitcher, double area fielder, and home run area fielders. Fielders cannot move from one area to another when a full team is playing. However, any number of players up to ten, can play Wiffle® Ball. When more than two players are playing, captains for each side are picked and they choose their respective teams alternately. As in baseball the game is played with one team at bat and one team in the field. The batting order of the team at bat shall be Pitcher 1st, then following the Catcher, Double area player, Triple area player and home run area player. The rules are similar to baseball. Three outs to an inning retire a side, nine innings to a game. In case of tie, additional innings are played. For a complete inning both sides must bat. An out for the batter can be made in three ways:

1. The batter can strike out only if he swings at a pitched ball and does not foul tip the third strike. Foul tips count as a strike for the first two strikes. A foul tip caught in back of the batter's box does not count as an out.

2. Fly balls caught in fair or foul territory.

3. Ground balls caught while ball is in motion in fair territory. Bunting is not allowed. The batter cannot obtain a base on balls.

SCORING —

Single markers are placed approximately 24 feet from home plate on foul lines. Ball hit in single area (i.e. area between batter's box and single markers) and not caught, constitutes a single. Double markers are placed approximately 20 feet in back of single markers on foul line. Ball hit in double area (area between single markers and double marker) and not caught, constitutes a double. Triple markers are placed on foul lines 20 feet back of double markers. Ball hit in triple area (area between double markers and triple markers) and not caught, constitutes a triple. Ball hit beyond the triple markers and not caught, constitutes a home run. The baseball rules of scoring apply. A player hits a single – his team has a man on first base (imaginary). The next player hits a single – his team now has an imaginary player on 1st. base and 2nd. base. The next player hits a home run – three runs score. The imaginary player on 1st and 2nd. and the home run. A player advances one imaginary base on a single, 2 bases on a double and 3 imaginary bases on a triple. A player on 2nd. base scores on a single, double or triple. A player on 3rd. base scores on any hit.

HOME RUN AREA

TRIPLE AREA

DOUBLE AREA

SINGLE AREA

FOUL LINE

FOUL LINE

THE RULES

What do a T-shirt, a Frisbee, and a palm tree have in common? They can all tell you when you've smacked a double. Pick a sport, any sport, and you'll be able to point to the official rules that help structure and govern the game. But for a solid game of Wiffle ball, all you really need is your gut and a little imagination.

The Mullanys wrote the official set of rules in 1953. Others featured in this book wrote their own too. But one of the things that continues to endear Wiffle ball to its aficionados is the great unspoken rule of Wiffle: You can make up or add rules to the game, as it serves your particular field, players, and creativity.

For many, it's the greatest thing about Wiffle ball. We've said it once, we'll say it again: It's a game that, more than most, belongs to its players.

That said, there are "official" rules. Pick the ones that work for you and build from there.

David A. Mullany says the most integral contribution to the brand, and the thing he is most proud of, is the official rules. He says it took days of painstaking deliberation to get them right. It was, indeed, a smart move to release the instructions/rules for the game at the time of the product's launch. Straight from their backyard in Fairfield, Connecticut, here are the official rules of Wiffle ball.

Even though these rules are available at wiffle.com, David A. estimates The Wiffle Ball, Inc. still snail mails a few hundred free copies of the rules each year to fans who request them from the Connecticut headquarters. "I think people think they're getting a little something extra by writing in," he says.

The only real difference from the original, official 1953 rules and the rules today are the descriptions of pitches. The "Out Curve" has become a "Curve," and the "In Shoot" is known today as a "Slider."

While these rules are great for some, others, especially those creating their own competitive leagues, have tweaked and shaped them to fit their own specifications. Here are some key additions and variations from some of the more competitive Wiffle organizations.

NEW JERSEY WIFFLE BALL ASSOCIATION

- Strike zone: metal sheet; 30 x 20 inches; mounted one foot off the ground.
- 75 to 85 feet from home plate to left field, 90 to 100 feet to center field, 75 to 85 feet to right field.
- Pitcher's mound: 42 feet from home plate.
- Pylons used as field markers.
- Games are four innings, with a 10-run mercy rule after two complete innings.
- No base running.
- Any ball that hits a pylon is a single.
- Double-Play rule: If the offensive team hits a ground ball with less than two outs in the inning, the defensive team may attempt a DOUBLE PLAY. The fielder must cleanly field the ball and throw and directly hit the strike-zone target.
- Tag-Up rule: With a runner on third base, if the batter hits a fly ball, the hitting team may yell "TAG" while the ball is still in the air. The fielder must throw the ball and hit the strike zone directly for a double play. If he/she misses the strike zone, the runner is safe.

The NJWA's strike zone.

WIFFLE UP!

- Medium-pitch mound is 41 feet from home plate; fast-pitch mound is 46 feet.
- Games are five innings, with a 10-run mercy rule after two innings.
- No base running.
- One and Done rule: If a batter does not swing and the pitch hits the strike zone on any one of the first three pitches, the batter is out.
- Tag-Up Rule: same as NJWA Tag-Up rule.

FAST PLASTIC

- Strike zone: 27 x 23 inches, and 13 inches off the ground.
- Backstop is 8-foot square placed four feet behind home plate.
- Pitcher's mound: 45 feet from home plate.
- 75 to 85 to left field from home plate, 95 to 115 feet to center field, 75 to 85 feet to right field.
- No base running.
- Double-Play rule: Double plays are recorded when one fielder fields a ground ball cleanly. The fielder then must throw the ball to another fielder who has one foot on or inside the Double Play Depth (DPD), who must then throw the ball and directly hit the strike zone. Should the fielder catching the ball drop it, his/her only play to get an out is to throw the ball toward home to tag the runner at first base. All other runners advance one base.
- A double play can also be if "tag" is yelled on a fly ball with less than two outs. The fielder must catch the ball in the air and throw the ball directly to the backstop or strike zone to get the lead runner.

It's obvious that the above rules and set-ups have been given some serious thought. The beauty of Wiffle ball is that it's a DIY game. The key to any Wiffle ball field is simple: Use what you have. In making your own house rules, take under advisement those original 1953 rules, the "pro" league rules, and some basic traditional implements.

Any folding chair can double as a strike zone. A tree, a shirt, a house, a rock, a stick, a cone, a ball, a hat, a bag, a little brother—really anything can stand in for a field marker.

Home-run fences can also come in all shapes and sizes: a house, a gate, a rope, or a pole (laid flat)—even a body of water can serve as the boundary for home-run territory.

Why not make the top of the tool shed a grand slam? Or, if the batter hits the palm tree, it's an automatic double. What if the batter hits the bedroom window?: an automatic out. Wherever you decide to play, the possibilities are endless.

And it doesn't matter how many people you have.

Try some of these on for size and you'll soon figure out your own house rules. But always remember, get them straight *before* you play. ●

6 Fields

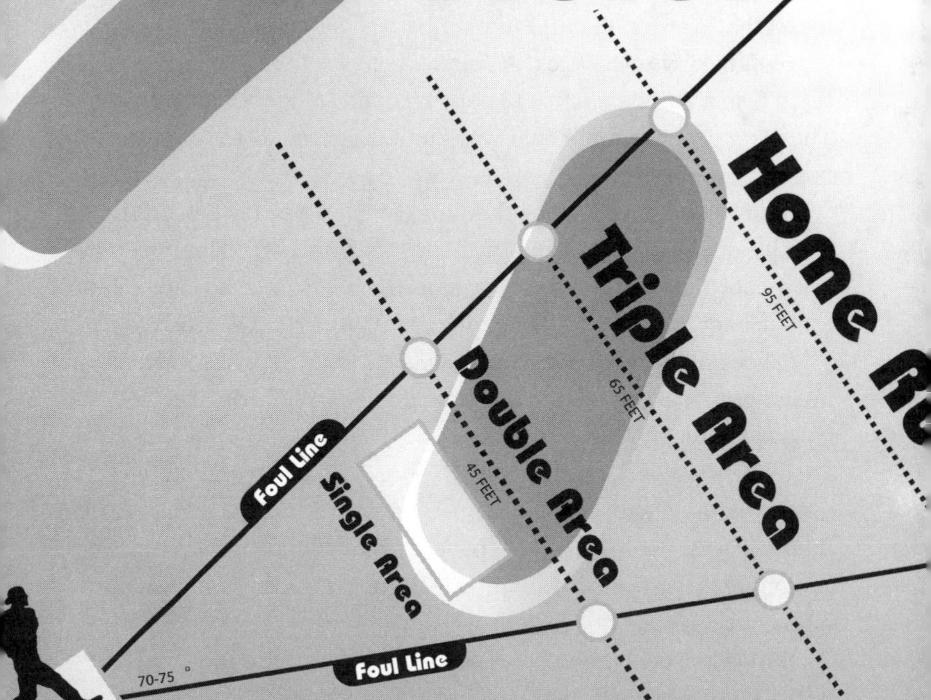

Home R
95 FEET
Triple Area
65 FEET
Double Area
45 FEET
Single Area
Foul Line
Foul Line
70-75 º

Growing up in Westchester County, New York, I played my fair share of Wiffle ball. My long-gone junior high, Briarcliff Middle School, had two of the greatest Wiffle fields around. One was our own "Fenway Park," a tiny field in a tucked-away place behind the outdoor basketball court. Our Fenway was made of dirt and hardly what you'd call cavernous. In fact, it was like playing in a small, concrete box. The right-field wall was a four-story, yellowish stone monster—it was right on top of you—and was the kiss of death for a left-handed pull-hitter like me. Ground rules stated that fielders could catch any ball hit off that wall for an out. What a rip-off.

Left field was the trick. As high as the white bricks were stacked, there was always a chance to pop one over. And I did occasionally. The glory? I got to run all the way around the school to retrieve the ball on the other side.

Our other field, "Yankee Stadium" may as well have been the Grand Canyon. That was on the near side of the school between the town pool and the tennis courts. In all the years I played there, I never hit one over the long, black, chain-linked fence. It still bugs me.

Those fields were ready-made, places where space, obstacle, and imagination came together. So what makes a Wiffle ball field a Wiffle ball field, anyway?

Wiffle ball was meant to be played in backyards and other congested areas. The ball was designed *not* to travel far. If you have more than 100 feet, you're wasting space. Each field has its own unique "automatics." In our neighborhood, "Joe's Car" was always an automatic out.

Wiffle ball fields come in all shapes and sizes. The most popular field marker is probably either a T-shirt or a Frisbee. Worst obstacle:

a swimming pool. For a strike zone, many people use a chair, but others use a pitch-back. Still others use a tin rectangle and some use a net.

One of the great things about a Wiffle ball field is that it's yours, and the rules are, there *ain't no* rules. The white ball and the yellow bat are standard, but beyond that, it's played in schoolyards and backyards, in malls and on battlefields. Like a Christmas tree, it's yours to decorate.

And then there are other fields, fields of legend among Wiffle ballers. After some painstaking consideration, these are my best-ever Wiffle ball fields, and the fanatics behind them.

STRAWBERRY FIELD

Strawberry Field is the brainchild of prolific Hollywood talent manager Rick Messina. Messina manages or has managed some of the biggest talent in comedy—names like Tim Allen and Drew Carey. His home in Encino, California, in the San Fernando Valley, and the field he built there beginning in 1997, have become a veritable temple to Wiffle.

The ex-New Yorker took his devotion to Wiffle ball to a new level, not only turning his own backyard into a Wiffle field of dreams, but buying his neighbor's house in order to do it up right.

That's a Wiffle ball fanatic.

A visit to Rick's ranch-style spread is like walking into a serious sports fantasy. It starts with the media room

Strawberry Field from the center-field seats.

Kenny Albert

Football and baseball play-by-play announcer for FOX television, radio voice of the New York Rangers and the New York Knicks

. . . On playing Wiffle ball in New York City.

In college at NYU I lived in a dorm on University Place downtown, right in the Village called Weinstein, right on 8th and University. There were two towers: the front tower when you first walked in, and one across the courtyard, the back tower.

The courtyard in the middle was the perfect Wiffle ball set-up and we used to have games there all the time. It was the perfect setting. It was the perfect size. And this was back in the '80s, and I'm at a dorm in Manhattan. It's not like you're in college with a big campus, [like] Wisconsin, Maryland, or Michigan or one of the other places where you had fields. You really had to think out of the box if you wanted to have some athletic activity in New York City.

I can still picture the way it was set up in between these two towers. It was a perfectly sized courtyard for Wiffle ball. The entire back wall of the front tower and the entire front wall of the back tower all [faced] the field. Our room was in the back tower and the windows would face the middle of the courtyard so there were always some interesting moments when people let their shades up. If you remember, during the Mets' runs in '86 and '88 [the] fans at Shea Stadium were putting up Ks for Doc Gooden for every strike-out. What was funny to us at the time is that these guys in the dorm who weren't playing started hanging up the Ks out of the windows in the courtyard while we played Wiffle ball. It was hysterical.

That courtyard was the perfect size for Wiffle ball and what really stands out was that "K corner." Those guys would hang up the sheets and towels out the windows. They would have the forward Ks for the regular strikeout and the backward K for the called-looking. It was like it was Doc Gooden out there.

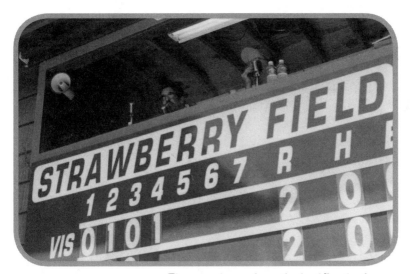

The press box: where the heckling begins.

(which is inside the main house and lines the left-field wall of the field), and continues with the suspended press box above home plate. The house next door has been converted into a clubhouse with showers, along with a game room. There's even a pub, basketball court, badminton court, horseshoes pit, and a pool.

And then there's the field itself, the crisp green Sport Court glistening in the Southern California sun. The stands above the field have played host to a who's-who of entertainment luminaries. Behind home plate is an unforgiving slab of tin that dings, pings, and pungs to proclaim a strike.

Sure, Rick had a few bucks, he had time, and he had the dedication to get the details right. What is it about Wiffle ball that appealed to him?

"I'm one of these guys that fights growing old. Most people that know me think I'm a big kid. And I'm north of 50, so Wiffle ball was a perfect activity. "

A one-of-a-kind Wiffle ball field.

Between 1997 and 2000, Rick built Phase I of Strawberry Field. The neighborhood filled with the sound of backhoes and cement mixers as he dug up and filled in a pool (a certifiably crazy thing to do by Hollywood standards) and built a concrete wall to give his next-door neighbor some privacy, as well as a respite from the sounds of plastic on plastic.

The thing was, in Rick's mind, it could have been better. There was just one teensy, tiny obstacle: his neighbor, or rather, his neighbor's house. The neighbor had been very accommodating, but the edge of his house overhung Rick's field slightly, spoiling the sightlines and even, heaven forbid, encroaching (slightly) into fair territory.

His field was good, not great. Still, the wall would come in handy—for seats!

"It was the kind of thing where when you do it a little bit, you start thinking about *what if*, and that's all it was. In other words, *I had the wall, what if I put in a railing? Oh, wow, a railing and a wall. What if we put seats? Wow, we've got a railing, a wall, and seats. Now the lights.* Then I said, 'Okay, we have foul poles, we need fair screens.'"

Q

Which former New York Yankee appeared in the first and only Wiffle TV commercials?

Then came an unexpected crisis. After all the work Rick had put into his dream field, the next-door neighbor put his house on the market. "I kept thinking, *If he sells it, I have no guarantee who he sells it to. And there's a really good chance I won't have a guy who is as accommodating as he was.*" So in 2000, he bought the neighbor's house.

Once he got the new house, he put in the booth, scoreboard, wall, the placards, and right field. "I blew it out and opened it up." Rick removed a whole section of house that jutted into fair territory, and Strawberry Field began to take its final shape.

To fill the stands, ordinary seats wouldn't do.

Rick has collected stadium seats from all over—seven Meadowland seats, 16 "Big A" seats, and 12 from Edison Field.

Then there are the monitors. There are monitors in the dugouts, monitors in the game rooms on either side of the field proper, there are monitors everywhere. "You've got the monitor right here for balls and strikes so you don't have to look down. You've got your technician sitting here. We've got a pitcher camera, a fielding camera. You can take phone calls, have a drink. We have a locker room, we got cubbies, we got the phone, and we got the bat rack. The electric scoreboard control is here so the bench team keeps track of the electric scoreboard," Messina says.

There's even a PA system second only to Yankee Stadium's, and on game nights there are even vendors selling bags of peanuts.

So who plays here? Largely Messina and his buddies. It depends on who's in town. "I get e-mails from Saudi Arabia and I have to tell them it's

Whitey Ford, in 1961.

just a bunch of comics and writers playing pick-up. Let me put it this way: I consider myself blessed because I'm in a stupid business. It's given me this."

And remember, because Rick's friends are comics and writers, game night can get pretty rough, from the jeers and catcalls of the rowdy fans in the stands, to the flawless Harry Caray-imitating announcers, comedians Jeff Hatz and Jeremy Kramer, who may be the best hecklers in the game. "It's like a roast as much as it is a play-by-play. It is brutal for a visiting team to come in and not realize they are going to be personally humiliated when they come to the plate," Messina says.

Still, there are perks to take the sting out of the home crowd's abuse. "If you're the visitors, you've got a dugout and a locker room, yeah. And a masseuse. That's right," he said, "a masseuse." And then there's the bar, a fully tricked-out, state-of-the-art temple-within-a-temple, dedicated to knocking back a cold one or three. If you didn't know you were in a Wiffle ball mecca in Encino, you'd swear you were in a real pub. Messina put in "a triple sink, ice machines, the whole nine yards." Not a bad choice of tap beers, either.

Messina refuses to add up his all-in costs, but a betting man would say it's more than a few-hundred-thousand dollars.

Did he know he was building not just a ball field but a legend? Messina himself seems baffled by the renown of his dream field.

"I mean, I'm still working in this stupid [show] business. So I'm still pitching projects and trying to sell shows. Every time I go into a pitch meeting at a network, all they want to talk about is the stupid Wiffle ball stadium."

Perhaps Rick's friend Jon Borchers sums it up best: "You know, it's funny. We take this more seriously than our regular lives." It shows.

Steve Turro admires his master-
piece from right-center field.

OX FIELD

Steve Turro is a phys ed teacher in northwestern New Jersey. He
looks like a ballplayer. Squint hard enough and he might even look like
a guy with a crazy dream who got on a bulldozer and turned a stretch
of New Jersey woods into a little piece of Wiffle ball heaven. He calls it
OX Wiffle Grounds, and since 1991 it's been his own field of dreams.

Steve has a wife, Mia, and three kids. They live in the sleepy
town of Wantage. A second baseman, he played in college and even
a little semipro ball. Turro is also a lifelong Wiffle ball player. He says
it made him a better baseball player. "I learned to switch-hit playing
Wiffle ball. If there's a tree in left field, you had to bat lefty. That's how
I learned to hit the ball that way."

Wiffle ball was and is his passion. Even when they were dating,
Steve told Mia about his lifelong dream of building a Wiffle field in
his backyard. When they searched for a house, the various prospects'

suitability for a Wiffle field was the priority, not nearby schools or distance to work.

"I thought, *My husband's nuts*," Mia said.

Finally, they found the house with all the backyard they needed. The problem was, that backyard looked more like a forest. Just two days into his newly minted marriage, Steve brought in the bulldozers. Two months later, OX Field was born.

There's a romance to this endeavor you won't find anywhere else. Just as in a certain Kevin Costner film, Steve cleared the land, planted the grass, put up the lights, named it OX Field after his dad, who worked like an ox...and they came.

Each year, OX Field has evolved. "It became a hobby. Some people build model airplanes, I did this," he said.

His "hobby" field *really* started getting serious when he tried to make it play like Yankee Stadium. "I took the dimensions from Yankee Stadium from 1976. I took those dimensions that were real short in right, deep in left center." Steve's field is 75 feet down the right-field line, 96 feet to right center. And how did he arrive at those measurements?

DID YOU KNOW

The original Wiffle ball which went on sale in 1953 is identical in size to today's Junior Size Wiffle ball.

"Algebraically. I scaled it down…I did that through a series of experiments to see how far one went if you really cranked it. I established that a 100-foot Wiffle shot was roughly equal to a 380-foot baseball shot." And, he maintains, the markings are "dead on."

"Some people build model airplanes, I did this," Turro said.

OX Field has 25-foot foul poles, lights, real bases, a scoreboard and a bat rack full of personalized bats. The bases just are there for show. There's a doubles line. The track or the fence on the fly is a triple.

His friends and family are a hard-playing bunch, and like any passionate group of Wiffle players, they've had their share of controversies. All high-level disputes are settled at winter meetings—just like in the bigs—and new rules would then, and only then, be added to Steve's 25-page rulebook."

Turro says playing Wiffle ball in his field of dreams is like "a live video game." Even in his forties, he is still just a kid at heart, dreaming he's Graig Nettles, Hideki Matsui, or A-Rod. Steve's wife, Mia, has an interesting perspective.

"I've met people who have met people who have met people who have [played] here. I'm a nurse and have had patients who will be like 'Wait a minute, you have that ballfield in Sussex county? I had a cousin who was at your house,'" she said.

It's one man's sports fantasy, one which he's in no hurry to share with the whole world. "I'm not exactly the kind of guy who wants to go around publicizing [this place]. But after 18 years, everybody knows it's here. The standard reaction is, 'I can't believe that' when they actually come down and see it," he says. "I haven't met too many guys who haven't thought this was the greatest thing in the world."

Picture Show Park at
the Pineyards.

PICTURE SHOW PARK AT THE PINEYARDS

In Winnetka, Illinois, in the north suburbs of Chicago, there's a Wiffle
ball field like no other. It isn't the most glamorous field or the most
state-of-the-art. But what it is may be the field that best captures the
Wiffleness, the pure spirit of Wiffle ball.

Picture Show Park at the Pineyards is the pride and joy of Mike
Leonard. Mike, a correspondent for *The Today Show*, is a transplanted
New Yorker. He's 62 years old and the father of four.

And it's his front lawn. It's *just* a front lawn, and yet, and yet…

Every Sunday, with real (and removable) foul poles and distance
markers, regular players, a remote-controlled electronic scoreboard,
and even a monument in center field, a Wiffle ball field takes shape.
Mike's 25-year-old son, Brendan, and his friends, the neighbors, and
sometimes Bob Costas come over and play some of the best Wiffle ball
going. And it stops traffic.

Mike started playing Wiffle ball when Brendan was 12. And the darned thing just grew. "It's like anything in life. Little things loom large. Like a father and his son can maintain a relationship on it with this quasi-serious fantasy sport. We've taken a front yard and just made it into this really cool stadium."

Mike carries all this off with a great deal of panache and with tongue planted firmly in cheek. In fact, if you search "Wiffle ball" on YouTube, near the top of the list will be Mike's homemade master-piece on Picture Show Park. Simply put, these Wiffle games let Mike hang out with the kids and the kids hang out with Mike. "This is my golf, this is my NASCAR, this is my fishing."

Funny or not, you'd think the neighbors would have a problem with a traffic-stopping Wiffle ball field right smack in the middle of their quiet suburban community. But because it's portable and can be put up and taken down quickly, the neighbors are cool. "We have holes in the ground, so we have this fence with these posts that stick in, and it all goes together. And we have an artificial mound. I can set it up in 15 minutes. Then people go, 'Here it is. Here's the stadium.'"

There were adjustments to be made. "We had to yank a tree in right field out. And it's funny because it was the tree my daughter planted on Earth Day. It's not the greatest thing to do. My daughter forgave me…she likes the stadium way better."

Far from being a nuisance for the neighbors and family, it's some-thing for them to be proud of. "And I'm that crazy guy with the field," says Leonard. "I can hit a Wiffle ball as far as Manny Ramirez can hit a Wiffle ball. One of the great parts about it is, you don't have to be big and strong. It's just a perfect com-bination of fantasy and reality, sports with competition."

This is my golf, this is my NASCAR, this is my fishing.

And it's crazy how people show up, like Costas, an NBC colleague. "He came by with

Bob Costas
Broadcaster and host, *NBC Sports*, *MLB Network*

. . . On the variations of baseball.
Every kid of my generation, at least every baseball loving kid that I know, played variations of baseball. You played stickball, you played softball, you played slap ball, punchball. To me, there are more variations on baseball than any other sport, including board games. Strat-O-Matic, or back in the old, primitive days, Ethan Allen baseball where you spun a dial. I think things that allowed at least people of our generation to simulate the feel of baseball.

. . . On what makes Wiffle special.
It can be a fantasy game, you know. To me, it's just always felt like another fun way to simulate baseball, especially in a confined space. It's something that you can enjoy and be competitive at but also not take seriously at the same time. You can make the ball dip and swerve and do crazy stuff. That's what makes it great.

. . . On growing up with Wiffle ball.
In the imagination of a kid, [any space] looked like the regular dimensions of a ballpark of our youth. You know, you have the telephone pole over here, and the neighbor's fence over there, and the hedges over here, and they become reasonable dimensions of a quirky ballpark. Maybe the stoop or the back porch is home plate so that when a pitch is taken or a pitch and miss, it's not going too far. It's just kind of whatever, however many you got.

. . . On traveling across state lines for a Wiffle ball game or two at Picture Show Park at the Pineyards.
There's always kind of a tongue-in-cheek aspect to Wiffle ball. My son, Keith, went with me, and it's an amazing thing. [Owner] Mike [Leonard] lives in this idyllic neighborhood outside Chicago, where neighbors walk and wave to one another. He calls it, "the Wiffle Ball Field of Dreams." It's just a perfectly quirky thing.

his son, played a few games. He started *announcing* when he wasn't playing. And a neighbor said, 'I saw you guys playing last night and someone sounded *exactly* like the host from the Olympics.' Well, that *was* the host of the Olympics. Costas picked up on the same stuff that makes it so cool.

"Part of this magic that we believe exists in this game lies in our imagination. To a lot of people who think it's really childish, but it's more childlike, which is a better way of putting it, I think."

Pat O'Connor's cathedral: Little Fenway.

LITTLE FENWAY

Pat O'Connor is a longtime manager at IBM. He lives in Jericho, Vermont. He just plain loves baseball, like millions of other ordinary fans. But Pat's an extraordinarily motivated guy, and his extraordinary creation, a Wiffle ball field called "Little Fenway" has given something special to more people than he ever could have imagined.

The Green Monster looms in the background at Little Fenway.

O'Connor has long been involved in baseball. He's coached Little League; umpired Little League, high school, American Legion, and college games; and he's played slow pitch softball for 20 years.

Still, he yearned to be closer to the game. He would say that the inspiration to build a baseball field in his backyard would come in moments of solitude and develop over time. Ultimately, he decided to build a one-fourth-scale version of Fenway Park in his backyard. Why Fenway? Because it's just such a cool ballpark.

From a sketch on a napkin, he and his friends turned his backyard into a killer version of the American League landmark, complete with its very own Green Monster and Citgo sign, each a mile high. They built a deck in center field to hold 10 seats for fans, just like the real Fenway's cheap seats. There are even tomato plants—yep, just like Fenway's.

In total, Little Fenway, from construction through its first season, cost $9,500 and officially opened for game play on the Fourth of July 2001. People started coming to play or just to see the park. The fame of Little Fenway spread. It was featured in *Sports Illustrated*, *Esquire*,

Travis Roy

. . . On Pat's tournament.

We just got a call from Pat, and he told me he read my book, *11 Seconds*. He asked if he could do a fundraiser for the Travis Roy Foundation. So we put together a tournament. I think we had six teams that year. It was a round-robin and we raised about $4,000. It was just a great, great event.

. . . On Pat O'Connor.

Pat's one of these people who gets excited. It's like meeting Santa Claus. It's one of those things that makes the [event] weekend as fun as it is, just to have everyone at his house. He gets such pleasure out of seeing people enjoy playing Wiffle ball. And he's a baseball nut.

. . . On the excitement.

I've never seen an event that's come up after eight years where the energy gets better every year. It's the same people. They can't wait just to be there and watch the games. There's so much camaraderie, and the bonus is that there's a nice balance between the competitiveness on the field and the competitiveness off the field to raise money. People get it. I'm very fortunate.

For more information on the Travis Roy Foundation and charity tournament, visit www.travisroyfoundation.org

Little Wrigley sits just behind Little Fenway in O'Connor's backyard.

Little Wrigley

To capitalize on Little Fenway's popularity, O'Connor built a Little Wrigley on his property, directly behind Little Fenway. It was completed in 2007. Tom O'Connor, Pat's father, put the last brick in the Little Wrigley wall, a real brick from Chicago's Wrigley Field. With an American League park and a National League park on the same property, O'Connor reasons that he has doubled the opportunities to do some good.

O'Connor's fields share in the magic of their major league counterparts. Little Wrigley's clock is set an hour earlier than Little Fenway's, on Chicago time, and Little Wrigley is even growing ivy.

and *Maxim,* among other publications. O'Connor, a lifelong Angels fan, found himself embraced by Red Sox Nation.

From the first moments, the field was a labor of love, a beautiful thing in its own right. O'Connor found, as he thought he might, the Zen of ballfield ownership. While other guys might see cutting their backyard grass as a chore, he actually wanted to be a groundskeeper. He even hired a professional groundskeeper to show him how—a guy who'd worked several Super Bowls. His wife, Beth, says Pat simply likes watching the grass grow.

Then fate took an at-bat. After 9/11, Little Fenway held a game for the local Little League that doubled as a fundraiser for the recent 9/11 victims. They raised over $1,400 and a light went on: Little Fenway is great venue for charity events. Since 2002, Little Fenway has helped to raise money for the Jimmy Fund, the Amyotrophic Lateral Sclerosis (ALS) Association of New England, and the Jared Williams Foundation. It's also been a destination for local organizations, including teen centers, grocery stores, the University of Vermont, and local high school graduations.

Among all its charitable associations, Little Fenway has been most involved with the Travis Roy Foundation. In 2002, O'Connor held the first-ever Travis Roy Foundation Wiffle Ball Tournament. By 2006, it had grown into a 16-team, three-day competitive tournament. In total, Pat has raised nearly a million dollars through the years for the foundation—all through Wiffle ball games.

"For me it's the look on people's faces when they first come up, the first time they've been here. That's by far at the top of my list. That 'wow' factor. That 'Gee, I've got to call my wife or my dad' factor. The 'I can't believe this' factor. Some say it's the eighth wonder of the world."

O'Connor, a lifelong Angels fan, found himself embraced by Red Sox Nation.

HONORABLE MENTIONS

There are a few other fields that deserve honorable mention.

Rookies

For $50 per hour, Cheeseheads can take their best swings at Steve
Schmidtt's Rookies Food & Spirits in Mazomanie, Wisconsin.
Schmidtt, himself, goes on record saying the palatial field in his bar's
backyard is the only official artificial-turf Wiffle ball field in the land.

Big League Dreams

Big League Dreams is a 40,000-square foot, Wiffle-only facility, borne
from an indoor ice skating rink in Medford, New Jersey. Co-owner Pat
Douglas says they specialize in children's Wiffle ball parties. Though,
Douglas says, "the dads that come in enjoy it just as much—if not
more—than the kids who come in here."

Rookies' artificial-turf Wiffle ball field.

Studio 42

One of the most beautiful Wiffle ball fields you'll ever see is located in Secaucus, New Jersey, of all places. In 2008, Major League Baseball moved in to the old MSNBC digs and transformed them into their own state-of-art studio for their hot-off-the press MLB Network. There, on the former Keith Olbermann set, is a bright green swath of heaven known as "Studio 42," after Jackie Robinson's number.

MLB Network calls Studio 42 a "replica baseball field," but it is also acknowledged as "the best Wiffle ball field ever." The half-scale field-turf infield and pitcher's mound 30 feet from home plate, doubles as the set for Bob Costas' eponymously titled show, *Studio 42*. There is a replica outfield wall. There are bleachers and an out-of-town scoreboard modeled after the one in Philadelphia's Citizens Bank Park. There's even a "No Pepper" warning on the brick backstop to complete the effect.

Nice, but what's Studio 42 doing in this book? Here's a secret. Though MLB Network's motto is "Our National Pastime All the Time," the truth is closer to "Our National Pastime, Most of the Time, *Because We're Really Serious About Our Wiffle Ball*." The crew and on-air talent out at Secaucus are Wiffle ball fiends, with host Bob Costas taking his cuts alongside network president Tony Petitti.

With its state-of-the-art monitors and climate-controlled atmosphere (not to mention its huge light bill) Studio 42 may be, inch-for-inch, the most expensive Wiffle ball field ever built. ⚾

7

Science

What does a pitched Wiffle ball have in common with a Barry Zito curveball or a Roger Federer topspin forehand? Why, as some may argue, is it harder to hit the Wiffle ball than the others? The simple answer, as every Wiffler knows, is: it curves. Says so right there on the box. It curves like crazy. It curves whether you throw it with spin or without.

To put the Wiffle ball's famous curvy reputation into perspective, consider this: On its 60 foot, six inch flight to home plate, a good major league curveball will break as much as 14 inches. Executed well, by a highly trained, (not to mention highly paid) professional ballplayer, this ball is hard to hit. The comparable Wiffle ball pitch, covering a shorter distance of 42 feet, will break as much as *four feet* on its way to the batter, according to Fox Sports Net's *Sports Science*, making it devilishly hard to get even a small piece of it. *That's curvy*.

Okay, so anyone who's picked up a yellow bat knows that a Wiffle ball curves. But why does it curve? For a more detailed answer, we should ask that noted sports fan, Sir Isaac Newton.

Don't laugh, Newton was a major sports buff. Tennis was his game. He lived for it. And in 1672, Newton, while watching an early form of indoor tennis at Cambridge University, noticed that a hit tennis ball *spins* through the air. This was, for its time, an Earth-shattering observation—but Newton didn't stop there.

More important for our purposes, he noticed that as a ball spins, one side of the ball must have a faster velocity than the other. This, he figured, causes balls to curve through the air, often unpredictably. Just as we know that without Newton there'd be no gravity, without Isaac Newton, without this groundbreaking science, there'd be no baseball and *no Wiffle ball*.

Strangely enough, there came a time in American sport when no one thought a baseball curved in flight, that it was just an optical illusion. Curveballers like the legendary Dizzy Dean fought to prove their ball truly curved. Baseballs are mysterious concoctions made of cork, yarn,

Everybody knows a Wiffle ball curves. But why?

and leather, but it has been proven beyond doubt that they can be made to curve in the hands of a talented and practiced big-league pitcher.

Baseball and the physical science of baseball mechanics have been studied in considerable depth. The definitive work on the subject, *The Physics of Baseball*, by Robert Adair, Sterling Professor Emeritus of Physics at Yale University, is almost 20 years old.

As a baseball curves in flight, so too does a Wiffle ball. But why? Can science explain the effect the holes have on the ball's trajectory?

Let's look at a Wiffle ball.

It is a soft, white plastic sphere three inches in diameter and nine inches in circumference. It weighs 25 grams. Its most notable feature is its eight three-quarter-inch oblong perforations in one hemisphere.

It's lightweight, seamless but slotted, and hollow. Almost everything a baseball is not.

Unlike a baseball, a Wiffle ball curves without any strenuous arm action and without adding additional torque or spin on the ball.

Science has identified three forces that act on a Wiffle ball in flight.

The Wiffle ball.

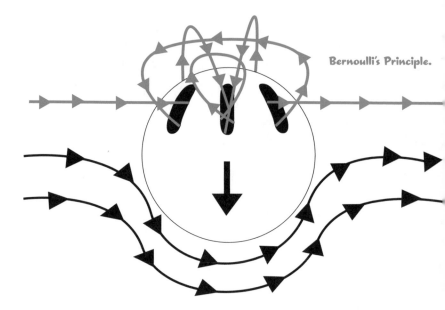

Bernoulli's Principle.

BERNOULLI'S PRINCIPLE

In the often cutthroat culture of big-league physics, marketing is frequently the edge a person needs to stand out and to win. Competition in the bigs is fierce. Careers are short, career-ending injuries common. It's more than just "publish or perish," you need a memorable moniker or a snappy catch phrase.

You get something named after you, it's like the Baby Ruth bar, a gift that keeps on giving. Planck's constant is a classic. Avogadro's number, one for the books, surely.

Having a number named after you was good. Sir Isaac Newton did those guys one better, though. He had *laws*—not hypotheses, not theories, but ironclad, indisputable laws.

Newton, the Father of Modern Science, kick-started something serious. Studying the behavior of objects in motion, he gave shape to a new field of science, what is nowadays known as physics. It was fertile ground for study and experimentation. Into this landscape came

Dutch-Swiss mathematician Daniel Bernoulli. He had a principle. And it was a honey.

In his 1738 book *Hydrodynamica*, he stated that "for an inviscid flow, an increase in the speed of the fluid occurs simultaneously with a decrease in pressure or a decrease in the fluid's potential energy."

Here it is in Greek:

$$\frac{v^2}{2} + \psi + \frac{P}{p} = \text{constant}$$

Got that? It's a hall of famer. For the sake of our discussion, air is a fluid. Bernoulli was the pioneer of fluid dynamics. It is his principle that best explains the lift created by an object in flight.

Taking into account adjustments for a fluid's gravitational potential (ψ) and density (p) Bernoulli theorized that the relationship between velocity (v) and pressure (P) is inversely proportional. For a fluid flowing horizontally, (air, for example), the highest velocity occurs where the pressure is lowest (in the case of an airplane above the wing) and the lowest speed occurs where the pressure is highest (below the wing). Thus, a simple pressure differential creates lift.

DID YOU KNOW

One of David A.'s first jobs was taping up bat handles in the Wiffle factory in Shelton, Connecticut.

A thrown Wiffle ball, having two asymmetric halves (and thus, by Bernoulli's principle, two different densities in its hemispheres), generates, among other forces, simple lift, by making air flow around its different halves at different rates, *even if the ball itself is not, in fact, spinning.* This is why, unlike a pitched baseball, a pitched Wiffle ball can actually *rise* on its way to the plate, adding a whole other dimension to the duel between pitcher and hitter.

Bernoulli's principle, the Wiffler's friend.

But wait, this is just the start of the science behind the Wiffle ball and its wicked curves.

THE MAGNUS EFFECT

In 1852, Henrich Magnus, a German chemist and physicist, took Newton and Bernoulli's findings a step further. He was studying the flight paths of cannonballs. He explained that a whirlpool of fluid, in this case, air, around a spinning object, creates a force perpendicular to the object's line of motion.

What does this mean? It means that when one side of the object moves faster than the other as it spins (thanks, Sir Isaac), it moves *down* as well as end over end. Ping-Pong players know this instinctively. Soccer players do too. To bend it like Beckham, you need to make it spin.

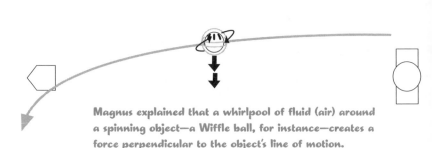

Magnus explained that a whirlpool of fluid (air) around a spinning object—a Wiffle ball, for instance—creates a force perpendicular to the object's line of motion.

The major league curveball is the best example. In baseball, as a curveball moves through the air from the pitcher to the batter, the ball's spin causes it to curve downward even as it continues to move forward. That's the Magnus Effect in action.

The Wiffle ball will curve with applied spin or without. The majority of Wiffle ball pitches have some spin on them, and the Magnus Effect plays its part in making the Wiffle ball do its swervy, curvy thing.

So what about those crazy holes?

THE OTHER MYSTERIOUS FORCES

The forces we discussed above, Bernoulli's Principle and the Magnus Effect act on Wiffle balls. They also act on soccer balls and baseballs and tennis balls. Uniform spherical objects, in other words. But since the Wiffle ball is hollow *and* made of lightweight plastic *and* perforated by eight oblong holes in one of its hemispheres, there are additional forces at work than can be seen with those other objects.

Many a Wiffler will tell you: It's the *holes, man*.

It may be hard to believe, but there are academics hard at work studying the Wiffle ball.

Fluid mechanics professor Jenn Rossman, PhD, of Lafayette University in Easton, Pennsylvania, is one of them.

A big baseball fan, her day job is to study and teach about the flow of matter. One practical example of fluid mechanics in action: understanding blood flow within veins and arteries can help doctors predict the probability of their patients developing aneurisms or having heart attacks.

Draped in her professorial white lab jacket, she explained that there are, in fact, other areas where fluid mechanics come in handy. Like why a Wiffle ball curves. Rossman has now spent the better part of five years studying the effects of putting a Wiffle ball in a controlled wind tunnel and observing its motion.

Jenn Rossman, PhD

Professor and Scientist

What do you study for a living and what do you teach?
I study fluid mechanics, which is anything that flows. One of the areas that I've studied for a long time is blood flow and the dynamics of how blood flow can tell you whether a certain artery is going to get clogged up with plaque, for example.

Another sort of interesting flow to me is the flow over a baseball. And it always interested me at first that people didn't believe the curveball is real. When I was a professor at Harvey Mudd College, we studied baseballs in a wind tunnel and would spin them with different rotation rates, about different axes, and see if we could measure the forces and if we could quantify the curveball effect.

Jenn Rossman, PhD and colleague explore the science behind the Wiffle ball.

It's called the Magnus Effect. It happens on any spherical projectile that's not totally symmetrical, or that has some spin on it. So, the idea is if it's spinning, you're going to get a force on the ball because of the spin. When you put a little backspin on a pitch, you effectively cause the airflow relative to the ball to be faster above the ball than it is beneath the ball. That backspin makes the velocity difference, the air-speed difference, which corresponds to the pressure difference. So, what you end up with is higher pressure pushing on the bottom of the ball. And so there's a net upward force on the ball because of the backspin you put on. That's the Magnus Effect.

[Then it was suggested that she study the behavior of a Wiffle ball.] What did you find?
We found we could make the Wiffle ball curve or rise without putting any spin on it, just by where the holes are relative to the air when you throw it.

You went into the study with some assumptions?
My assumption was the holes caused the Magnus Effect—a built-in Magnus. When the air goes over the holes it's effectively transferring over to turbulence. All that means is the air is going a little bit faster there, and so that's where there'll be lower pressure and a force toward the holes. That was my assumption.

How do you go about studying a Wiffle ball?
I'm in a lab and we're using a wind tunnel, which is a big fan that sucks air. We know that we've controlled that airflow.

The Wiffle ball is placed in the wind tunnel and it's tethered to something that's measuring the forces on it. Obviously, the air is going over it at the same speed that a real Wiffle ball would be flying through the air.

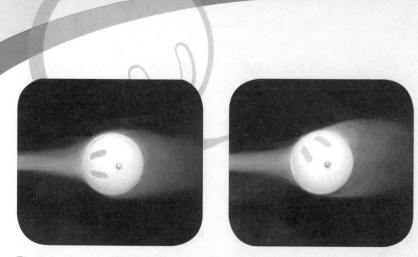

The behavior of a Wiffle ball varies with velocity, as well as the position of the holes.

So, you're emulating the distance between the mound and home plate as though it were a real pitch.
We're changing the pitching speed. The ball is not moving. It's basically on a spear in one spot in the wind tunnel. We're blowing air over it.

You have the Wiffle ball in the wind tunnel, on a spear. What sort of things are you looking for at this point?
We're looking at what the lift and the drag are on the ball. I tested pitch speeds from 10 miles per hour to 100 miles per hour. What happens to those forces as the air goes faster? What happens if the holes are up or down or on the side? Or straight forward?

What did you find at the different speeds?
There's a break point and it's at about 45 miles per hour. Beneath that speed, things acted one way, and above that speed, those relationships changed. So something is going on. I still don't know what it is with the changes there.

The airflow over the Wiffle ball is important and there is a Magnus Effect due to the holes, but there's also air flow inside the ball, which is not true for baseball. The airflow inside the Wiffle ball competes with what's happening outside the ball. And, so at the low speeds one of them dominates and at the higher speeds the other dominates.

It's way more complicated than David Mullany ever thought it was going to be. But it's pretty interesting.

Are you finding that ball is breaking more or less the faster you pitch?
If you want to do a sweeping generalization everything's stronger at higher speeds…with an asterisk [chuckling].

Wait, can I assume that asterisk includes scuffing and knifing the Wiffle ball?
Yeah, so there's external stuff that we don't know about, but what we definitely know from even the pristine balls is that when the air enters the Wiffle ball, the faster you're throwing it, the faster the flow is inside. It's not just flowing, it's forming a vortex inside the ball. In effect, two vortices. So two little whirlpools inside the ball. And, those cause another force on the ball. There's the force that's happening outside, the flow over the ball, and then there's this force due to what's inside the ball.

What is still mysterious at this point?
I think one of the missing things is the black art of scuffing and knifing. It just creates this whole other thing that tweaks everything.

Does that mean that scientists are ultimately going to become the best Wiffle ball players?
Well, I don't know if you've noticed the physiques of most scientists. That's probably not going to happen [chuckling].

Ryan Zimmerman

All-Star Third Baseman, Washington Nationals

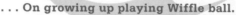

. . . On growing up playing Wiffle ball.

As I grew up and played baseball, I was playing on summer teams. You would play a baseball game earlier in the day and then you go out to the party afterwards and play Wiffle ball. So, I think it coincided with starting to play baseball.

We would play that if you got it to the pitcher before the guy got to first base, he was out. Or, you could obviously peg him. You could hit him before he got to first base [laughing].

. . . On playing on the beach.

I grew up right on the beach, and that's a pretty good place to play. There's obviously plenty of room and it's all sand and everything so you can dive and do whatever the hell you want. It's a lot of fun.

. . . On field markers.

We just had whatever we could find and used them as bases. And we didn't even have a strike zone. That was probably not the best way to do it. It definitely led to some arguments, but it's all part of the game, I guess you could say.

. . . On using dedicated field markers in the big leagues.

They could just kind of put a chair behind home plate and get rid of the umpire, right?

. . . On why he loves Wiffle ball.

Baseball is America's pastime and it's a lot easier to get a Wiffle ball and a bat and play. You don't need gloves, you don't need any of that. It's as close as you can get to baseball without playing baseball. All you need is a space, a ball, and a bat. It's just as much a part of America's pastime as baseball is.

You don't see as many kids just go out and play in the backyard or just be outside these days. Me and all my buddies had so much fun doing that, and it's a shame it doesn't happen as much as it used to.

One scientist who disagrees with some of Rossman's theories is Greg Culler, who writes for the MadSci Network, an online portal where scientists answer science questions from the public. Culler writes that the aerodynamics of the flight of a Wiffle ball are "pretty complex."

Many a Wiffler will tell you: *It's the holes, man.*

He emphasizes the effect of the holes in causing drag, the force that slows an airplane when the wheels go down. Culler says he believes, "The curve in the path of a Wiffle ball is driven more from an aerodynamic drag [wind resistance] perspective than the Magnus Effect."

"The holes are located on only one side of the ball to increase the drag on that side, causing the ball to curve toward the side with the holes... The holes are oblong to maximize this aerodynamic drag. If the holes were evenly distributed around the ball, the aerodynamic drag would be equal on both sides, and any curving would be the result of spin and the Magnus Effect."

Another academic with ideas about the Wiffle ball is Professor of Mathematics and codirector of the New York University Applied Mathematics Lab, Mike Shelley.

DID YOU KNOW

Professional Wiffle ball pitchers have been known to make a Wiffle ball break as much as four feet.

Shelley spends much of his time combining mathematical modeling and simulation with live experimentation. In other words, he figures out the best way to design things that bend in the wind in order to minimize their drag and make them more efficient.

He was not at all surprised that in spite of all the science inherent in the Wiffle ball, David N. Mullany did it the old-fashioned way.

"He built a body of informal and intuitive knowledge and he figured out how to do it. In other words, anyone can be a scientist, you just need curiosity. And good intuition requires good intelligence. It looks like Mr. Mullany had both."

The Wiffle ball is a scientific wonder that would make Sir Isaac Newton proud. So the next time you find yourself scuffing your ball on the concrete looking for that extra edge, you're not just scuffing up a Wiffle ball, you're showing Sir Isaac himself a little love. ●

Conclusion

This book has been a great journey from the dawn of physics to the golden age of industry and through the age of the iPod.

I wrote this book because of my own lifelong love of Wiffle—the game *and* the brand—and I hope I was able to instill a little of that love in you.

So the next time you pick up that familiar, half-punctured, rubbery white plastic orb, the next time you emulate "Derek Jeter" or "Grady Sizemore" armed with some classic yellow plastic in your backyard or at a Little Fenway of your own, I want you to remember that you're part of a great tradition. Remember Newton, remember Bernoulli. Remember Magnus and Mullany. Remember Palinczar and Piervinanzi, for goodness sake.

Most of all, remember that you're not just some suburban homeowner with a white plastic ball in your hand, you're a hero, a magician, a master of curving, swerving disaster, and in your hand, you're holding a legend. There's magic in that smooth white ball and its yellow sidekick.

The Wiffle ball may in fact be the great equalizer, but there is little that can equal the splendor of all this great game can offer. It will always live in the trunks of our cars, the space under our beds, behind the rakes in our garages, and most important, in our families' memories.

No one can guess what the next 60 years hold for Wiffle, but the same can be said of David N. Mullany and his 13-year-old son back in '53. So far, so good. When they talked at the kitchen table they could never have foreseen professional leagues coming. I believe that those leagues have real possibilities and they've done it by making them their own.

This interest has helped catalyze Wiffle squarely into social networking. And just maybe, someday, as an Olympic sport. No matter what, we'll always have the backyard.

What if all the world's problems could be settled with a friendly game? Think of it as "Wiffle ball Diplomacy." I challenge you to imagine a better way to resolve a dispute. Just think of those games: Brother vs. Sister. Union vs. Management. You get it. Maybe one day.

When I find myself plopped on the couch gazing numbly at my TV, I think of Central Park and Wiffle ball. Then soon enough, I'm out there throwing curveballs with a buddy.

It's been nice to see, up close and personal, in this 30 billion toy megaindustry, there's The Wiffle Ball Inc., looking in from the outside and smiling.

From humble beginnings, it is something that's brought joy to my life, and so many others. Here's to the Wiffle ball, an American classic.

—*Michael Hermann, January 2010*

Acknowledgments

My sincerest thanks to the dozens have made this book all it can be. Most of you know who you are—especially my folks.

Deep in the trenches:

My giant-sized thanks to Perrie Briskin, who coordinated, produced, and made this book go, go, go. It was nothing without her.

To my two great editors, Katy Sprinkel and Tony Puryear. Your tireless talents brought it all together.

Elliot Schaeffer and Matthew Zaklad, of course, and as always.

My research team headed by Zack Tawatari, Don Hermann, Frances Callaghan, Isaac Kim, and Allyson Klauber.

Chief photographer, Christopher M. Lynch of Instilled Images, and illustrator Ricardo Lopez. Thank you.

Gene Winter and Andy Corea of St. Onge Steward Johnston & Reens LLC for protecting and serving the Wiffle brand. Day after day after day.

An extra-special thanks to Mike Palinczar, Rob Piervinanzi, and Lou Levesque.

Samantha Merley and Louis Caffari for their innovative design elements.

And to Team Triumph: Mitch Rogatz, Tom Bast, and Don Gulbrandsen, and the sales and marketing team—thank you. For everything.

Of course, to my friends and colleagues offering their TLC:

Chris Golier, Bridget Fitzgerald, John Belus, Paul Hough, Glenn Petraitis, Peter Berkowitz, Matt Ricatto, Mike Fonseca, Ned Specktor, Carolyn Weyforth, Erika Alexander, Suzanne Metzger, Rich Taub, Eric Simon, Eric Hurwitz, Scott Debson, Jason Flom, Annmarie Swope, Sam Schlaifer, Elli Orlinsky, Yehuda Shmidman, Hud Giles, Doug Shenkman, Ahovi Kponou, Russell Thomas, Jill Zarensky, Robin Zarensky, Greg Werner, F. Noel, Daymond John, Mark Gullickson, Danielle Cohen, Joe Cohen, Carlos Huasipoma, Esther Min, Jimmy Zheng, Sally Traynham, Sean McKinney, Laura Newmark, Timothy J. Pastore, Brian Schnurr, Rob McGlarry, MLB Network, Rich Ticknor, MRT, Chris Isenberg, and to Rick Licht for planting the seeds.

And to those Wiffle fanatics who spent time talking with me about this great brand:

Julius Erving, Jim Bouton, Bob Costas, Nick Jonas, Muggsy Bogues, Kenny Albert, Ryan Zimmerman, Grady Sizemore, Gary Dell'Abate, Tim Kennedy, Connecticut Governor Jodi Rell, Gar Ryness, Jeff Griffing, Pat O'Connor, Travis Roy, Mike Alessi, Dave Ringler, Rick Ferroli, Steve and Mia Turro, Rick Messina, Mike Leonard, Team DOOM, Jenn Rossman, Ricky Comuniello, Brett Bevelacqua, Hank Paine, Chris Byrne, and Mike Shelley.

And to the Mullanys: David N., David A., David J., and Stephen. Well done.

Appendix: LEAGUE DIRECTORY

Multi-State

CT, MA, MO, NH, NJ, NY, OH, PA, RI
Wiffle Up!
www.wiffleup.com
info@wiffleup.com

MA, NJ, NY, PA
Golden Stick Wiffleball League
www.goldenstickwiffle.com
gswl@goldenstickwiffle.com

AZ, CA, FL, GA, IL, MA, MD, MO, NY, TX
Fast Plastic
www.fastplastic.net
nationalchampionship@fastplastic.net

CA
Bay Area Wiffle Ball
Oakland, CA
http://www.wifflebawl.com
raiders38002003@yahoo.com

CT
Big League Wiffle Ball
Guilford, CT
www.bigleaguewiffleball.com
info@bigleaguewiffleball.com

Prowiffleball
http://prowiffleball.wetpaint.com
natemuzza28@sbcglobal.net

DC
Potomac Wiffleball League
Washington, D.C.
www.potomacwiffleball.org
commissioner@potomacwiffleball.org

GA
Wiffle Atlanta
Decatur, GA
http://Wiffleatl.com
jk@wiffleatl.com

IA
Ottumwa Wiffleball
Southeast Iowa
http://www.ottumwawiffleball.com/
longs@ajiusa.com

IL
Stella's Wiffle Ball League
Lyons, IL
www.batcages.com/wiffle_ball.html
carey60534@aol.com

KS
Neighborhood Wiffle Ball League
Overland Park, KS
www.leaguelineup.com
    welcome.asp?cmenuid=1&url=wiffle-
    ball&sid=182426502
nsacommish@gmail.com

Pitt Wiffleball League
Pittsburg, KS
www.leaguelineup.com
    welcome.asp?url=pittwiffle
stucky1035tc@yahoo.com

MA
Auburn Wiffle Ball League
Auburn, MA
www.leaguelineup.com/welcome.
    asp?url=auburnwiff
golfman1390@yahoo.com

Cape Cod Wiffle Ball League
Cape Cod, MA
www.ccwbl.com
ccwbl.2006@yahoo.com

Galactic Wiffle League
North Dighton, MA
http://galacticwiffle.com
billrosby@gmail.com

HRL Massachusetts
Worcester, MA
www.hrlmass.com
thestevehrl@hotmail.com

New England Wiffle Association
Worcester, MA
www.newazone.com
staff@newazone.com

Wiffle Rock
Stoughton, MA
www.wifflerock.com
ca@wifflerock.com

MI
Fat Bastard Wiffle
Harvard Yards, MI
http://fatbastardwiffleball.com
fattywiffle@gmail.com

Kalamazoo Wiffle League
Kalamazoo, MI
www.kzoowiffleball.com
Join@KzooWiffleball.com

**Lake Orion Wiffle Ball
    Association**
Lake Orion, MI
http://lowa.wetpaint.com
rvandenboom@dgsd.k12.ak.us

MN
HRL Twin Cities
St. Paul/Minneapolis, MN
www.hrltwincities.com
deesnider@hrltwincities.com

NC
**North Carolina Wiffle Ball
    League**
Landis, NC
http://ncwiffleballleague.webs.com
ncwbl@hotmail.com

NJ
National Wiffle Ball League
Woodland Park, NJ
www.leaguelineup.com/nwbl
neighborhoodwiffleball@yahoo.com

**New Jersey Wiffle Ball
    Association**
Trenton, NJ
www.wiffleballusa.com
wiffleusa@aol.com

NY
Hess Field Wiffleball
Scotia, NY
http://hfwb06.tripod.com/index.html
chrishess@hessfieldwiffleball.com

Palisades Wiffle ball League
Rockland County, NY
www.palisadeswbl.com
info@palisadeswbl.com

OH
Pleasantview Wiffle League
St. Marys, OH
pleasantviewwiffle.tripod.com
helmstetter.5@wright.edu

OK
Oklahoma WiffleBall
Norman, OK
www.okwiffle.com
Chris.sanner@gmail.com

OR
**Columbia Cowlitz Wiffleball
    Association**
Portland, OR
www.leaguelineup.com/welcome.
    asp?cmenuid=1&url=ccwa&sid=
    182426502
nate.bullock@yahoo.com

PA
Backyard Wiffle Ball League
Wilkes-Barre, PA
www.leaguelineup.com/
    welcome.asp?url=bwbl-v2
backyardwiffleball@hotmail.com

**Langhorne Wiffleball
    Association**
Langhorne, PA
http://lwawiffleball.com
awaskie@lwawiffleball.com

TX
Cedar Park Wiffle (Fast Plastic, Austin Region)
Austin, TX
www.leaguelineup.com/welcome.
asp?cmenuid=1&url=TXWA&sid
=182360534
dean@cedarparktx.us

Lone Star Wiffle
Dallas, TX
www.leaguelineup.com/welcome.
asp?url=wifl
hooligan88@hotmail.com

VT
Southern Vermont Wiffle Ball League
Bennington, VT
www.myspace.com/SouthernVer-
montWiffleball
robmsvwl@comcast.net

Low Ball Wiffle
Lincoln, VT
www.lowballwiffle.org
architects@gmavt.net

WA
Seattle Wiffleball Association
Seattle, WA
www.leaguelineup.com/welcome.as
p?cmenuid=1&url=seattlewiffle&
sid=713374744
jcorson@wesleyan.edu

WI
Milwaukee Wiffle League
Milwaukee, WI
http://www.milwaukeewiffle.com/
milwaukeewiffle@gmail.com

Recreational Leagues

NH
NH State Wiffleball League
New London Recreation Department
New London, NH
www.nl-nh.com/index.asp?Type=B_
BASIC&SEC=%7B0CEF58E7-
41FE-4804-83F4-
1BC72E658011%7D
NHWL@live:com

NJ
Wiffle ball League
RiverWinds Community Center
West Deptford, NJ
www.riverwinds.org/
index.asp?Type=B_
BASIC&SEC=%7B6AFC1E92-
D85F-41FE-9DE4-
B5C6E431CAE2%7D
info@riverwinds.org

NY
Wiffleball Adult Coed League
City of Plattsburgh Recreation
Plattsburgh, NY
city-of-plattsburgh-rec.ezleagues.
ezfacility.com/leagues/55569/Wif-
fleball-Fall-Adult-Coed-League.
aspx
recreation@cityofplattsburgh-ny.gov

VA
Harrisonburg Adult Wiffleball League
Harrisonburg Parks and Recreation
Harrison, VA
www.findsportsnow.com/sports/
listing/8988/harrisonburg-adult-
wiffleball-league
Erikd@harrisonburgva.gov

About the Author

Michael innately understands the power of popular culture, creative media, and the art of business. His vision as the president of Wicked Cow Entertainment has elevated the company to its current position as the leading brand-strategy and business-development agency, with assets that have included the master licenses for The Notorious B.I.G., Julius Erving, and Wiffle, among others.

Michael's ability to identify, engage, and help shape cutting-edge brands lead him to Maxim and FUBU where he worked closely with the CEOs as a trusted advisor in both creative projects and business development.

His early career included stints as a local TV anchor and reporter, followed by a gig producing and hosting Fox Sports' *Reverse Angle*.

Michael received his B.A. in Journalism and Philosophy from the University of Wisconsin-Madison, and lives in good ol' NYC.

Photo Credits

4, 18, 63, 69, 85, 111, 118, 138: Getty Images

7: King Features

11: Rob Hoffman/JBE

12: Universal Uclick

13: Laura Goulet

17: The University of Connecticut/The Mullany
    Family

36–40, 42, 43, 45, 51, 58, 148: Christopher M. Lynch/
    Instilled Images

75, 78, 79, 93: Lou Levesque/Golden Stick Wiffle Ball

86: Dave Ringler

90–92, 94, 95, 97, 130, 132: Ricardo Lopez

108: Fox Sports

116: Mike Leonard

119, 120, 122: Pat O'Connor

124: Steve Schmidtt

125: MLB/Major League Baseball Network

134, 136: Jenn Rossman

Photos on pages 72, 80, 81, 102, 107, 109, 110, 113
    courtesy of the author.

All other illustrations and photographs courtesy of
    The Wiffle Ball, Inc.

Wiffle®, the images of the Wiffle® ball, and the
    Wiffle® Guys are federally registered trademarks
    of The Wiffle Ball, Inc., Shelton, CT 06484.

Library of Congress Cataloging-in-Publication Data

Hermann, Michael, 1970-
 Wiffle ball : the ultimate guide / Michael Hermann.
   p. cm.
 ISBN 978-1-60078-361-6
 1. Wiffle ball. I. Title.
 GV881.8.H47 2010
 796.357'8-dc22

                                    2010000888

This book is available in quantity at special discounts for your group or organization. For further information, contact:

Triumph Books
542 South Dearborn Street
Suite 750
Chicago, Illinois 60605
(312) 939-3330
Fax (312) 663-3557
www.triumphbooks.com

Printed in U.S.A.
ISBN: 978-1-60078-361-6
Design by Wagner Donovan Design